Ripley's Believe It or Not!

Vice President, Licensing & Publishing Amanda Joiner
Creative Content Manager Sabrina Sieck

Editorial Manager Carrie Bolin
Editors Jessica Firpi, Jordie R. Orlando
Junior Editor Briana Posner
Text Geoff Tibballs
Feature Contributors Engrid Barnett, Jessica Firpi, Jordie R. Orlando, Briana Posner
Factchecker & Indexer Yvette Chin
Proofreader Rachel Paul
Archivist Robert Goforth
Special Thanks to Ripley's Video Team Steve Campbell, Steph Distasio, Colton Kruse, and Matt Mamula

Designers Rose Audette, Luis Fuentes, Chris Conway
Reprographics Bob Prohaska
Cover Artwork Luis Fuentes

ISBN 978-1-60991-339-7

Manufactured in China in May 2020 by Leo Paper
First Printing

Library of Congress Control Number: 2020934647

PUBLISHER'S NOTE
While every effort has been made to verify the accuracy of the entries in this book, the Publisher cannot be held responsible for any errors contained in the work. They would be glad to receive any information from readers.

WARNING
Some of the stunts and activities are undertaken by experts and should not be attempted by anyone without adequate training and supervision.

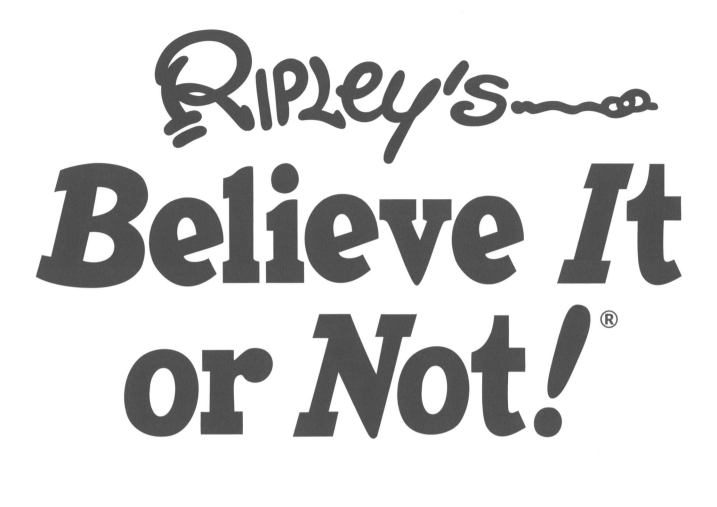

Ripley's Believe It or Not!®

MIND BLOWN! All TRUE & NEW

Ripley® PUBLISHING

a Jim Pattison Company

Ripley's Believe It or Not!

WHAT'S INSIDE

RIPLEY'S EXCLUSIVE

Exclusive interviews and photos you can only find here in this book!

inside the vault

Ripley's Believe It or Not! exhibits from deep within the vaults of our world-renowned collection.

FAN FEED

Unbelievable submissions from Ripley's fans all around the world.

THE MAN, THE MYTH, THE LEGEND

Robert Ripley was born in February 1890—a world without paper clips; basketball had never been played; the Coca-Cola Company didn't exist; and Vincent van Gogh was still alive. So when his humble job as a newspaper cartoonist snowballed into a life of globetrotting and celebrity, it was already unbelievable.

His iconic "Believe It or Not" cartoon led to him traveling to 201 countries—talk about #travelgoals—and reporting on every bizarre phenomena he encountered. Instead of a neon T-shirt emblazoned with the city name, Ripley was bringing home souvenirs like shrunken heads, tribal masks, Inuit whale harpoons, mammoth tusks, and Ming-period brass temple gongs.

In an era without social media, people bought more than 2 million copies of Ripley's first book, and in 1933, more than 2 million people took a gander through the first Ripley's "Odditorium" at the Chicago World's Fair. Craving more of his brand of unusual, his radio shows were a smash hit, and just as TV was taking off, Ripley had himself a TV show, too.

This is our history. This is the foundation of Ripley's Believe It or Not!

DUBAI ATTRACTION

In late 2019, a new Ripley's Odditorium graced the world at Global Village in Dubai, UAE.

The 31st Ripley's location and the first in the Middle East houses six galleries, thus carrying on the tradition of bringing you the world's most remarkable collection of oddities all gathered in one place.

The Odd Lives On ▶

Featured in *Ripley's Believe It or Not! Unlock the Weird!* for having the longest consecutive daily vlog and posting them to YouTube for 10 years, Charles Trippy has since gotten married and had his first child. Although he stopped filming daily to spend more time with his growing family, Charles is still sharing his love for Ripley's with his new baby.

COOL STUFF
STRANGE THINGS

The Ripley's YouTube series _Cool Stuff Strange Things_ is in its fifth season! And bringing you the most bizarre and odd stories (always with a twist of humor) are not one, not two, but four hosts— Sabrina, Adam, Steph, and Colton!

Together, the team covers everything from ancient teeth-whitening remedies and the horror of Cabbage Patch Kids, to the history of balloon animals and the real-life inspiration behind Pokémon characters! Learn more about the CSST team!

CAROLINA REAPERS

WEIRD

ROMANCE

Sabrina

Your OG host of _Cool Stuff Strange Things_. Enjoys edible props, from pork chops to string cheese—even crickets—but could do without another Carolina Reaper experience. Dislikes wearing hats, although the show's director/editor/magic maker always insists.

Colton

Not just a face of *Cool Stuff Strange Things*, but also the man behind the scenes—producing a plethora of Ripley's digital content, from Ripleys.com articles to the Notcast! Immune to brain freezes and possibly our resident nature expert, Colton is a Believe It or Not! himself. His favorite fact: Some moths can jam bats' echolocation as a defense against being eaten. Yum.

Steph

Ripley's pop culture maverick, bringing you all the bizarre about cannibal Cabbage Patch Kids and creepy toys like the Ouija board. If she finds a Believe It or Not! about the Jonas Brothers, that will for sure be next! But, the weirdest part of her day-to-day as Ripley's social media guru? Assisting online submissions of hands—well, photos of hands—touching our legendary fertility statues.

Adam

A Renaissance man of many skills, from web development to gaming commentary. Note the accent—he's your resident British *Cool Stuff* correspondent. But don't be surprised if he goes offtrack in episodes to come, doting on his passions for chicken "tendies" and pop punk.

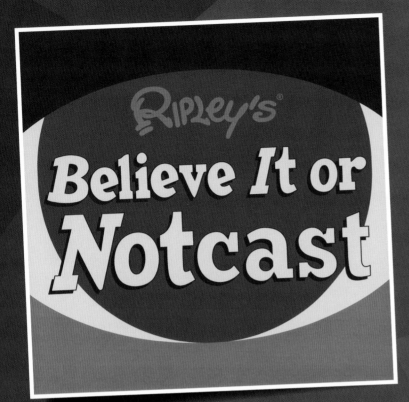

Believe It or Notcast

HEAR THE WEIRD!

Launching in 2019, the Ripley's Believe It or Notcast brings podcast listeners deep into the strange, the bizarre, and the unusual.

With episodes dropping weekly, hosts Ryan Clark and Brent Donaldson take you on a journey to the world's most off-limit places, talk with a modern-day witch in Salem, and even interview horror legend Bruce Campbell (aka host of *Ripley's Believe It or Not!* on Travel Channel)—plus so much more!

Available on iTunes, Spotify, or wherever you get your podcasts!

"Both Brent and I have loved Ripley's since we were kids, so we have a real respect for the brand and the way we tell stories here. We try to bring that respect and give an homage to the past in every episode."

—Ryan Clark

DIGITAL GET DOWN

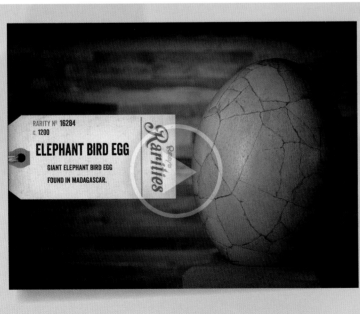

RARITY Nº 16284
c. 1200
ELEPHANT BIRD EGG
GIANT ELEPHANT BIRD EGG
FOUND IN MADAGASCAR.

Ripley's Rarities

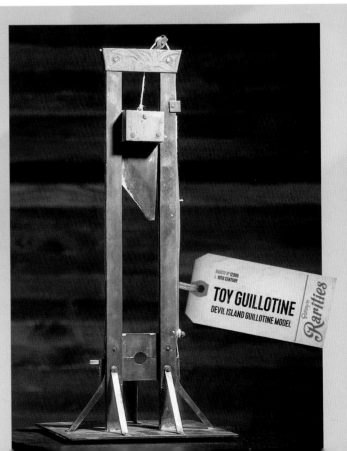

RARITY Nº 12899
c. 19TH CENTURY
TOY GUILLOTINE
DEVIL ISLAND GUILLOTINE MODEL
Ripley's Rarities

Ripley's Rarities

Still can't get enough from "Inside the Vault"? Ripley's Rarities takes you up close and personal with some of the most interesting exhibits in the Ripley's Believe It or Not! collection.

YOUR HOSTS

Brent

Brent Donaldson is a career magazine journalist whose features have covered true crime, cage fighting, the arts, politics, higher education, and the tech industry. Brent lives with his wife and two sons in Cincinnati, Ohio—scarring them daily with stories from Ripleys.com. Believe it or not, Brent was the last journalist ever to interview Evel Knievel!

Ryan

Ryan Clark is a journalist by trade and has published books and articles on a variety of topics; he's currently a university professor. Believe it or not, Ryan has hunted for ghosts in Civil War mansions, made bets at the Kentucky Derby with Gilbert Gottfried, chased hurricanes in Mississippi, and has driven a good portion of Route 66 to get to the International UFO Festival in Roswell, New Mexico!

CARNIVOROUS BUNNY RABBITS

JINGLE BELLS ISN'T A CHRISTMAS SONG

MANY BELIEVE THE SONG WAS ACTUALLY WRITTEN FOR THANKSGIVING.

RIPLEY'S BELIEVE IT OR NOT! — DECEMBER 25, 2019   SHARE ON: f ⬤ ⬤ t ⬤

Weird True Facts

Be sure to check out WTF—Weird True Facts! This weekly video series covers weird news, amazing animals, extreme nature, strange biology, vintage and historical oddities, and everything in between.

Or Not!

Every week brings a new OR NOT! With more than 130 misconceptions, myths, and modern-day "facts" debunked since the series first started, OR NOT! continues to turn your world upside down, because you can't always... Believe It!

DYED DOGS

Anaïs Hayden of Atlanta, Georgia, takes dog grooming to a whole new—and colorful—level!

With a brush in one hand and a pair of grooming shears in the other, Anaïs can transform your average pooch into a Lisa Frank–inspired masterpiece or even a different species! Some of her impressive makeovers, which take anywhere from three to six hours, include trimming and dying a dog's fur to make them look like zebras, giraffes, tigers, panda bears, and even betta fish!

Anaïs got into the creative dog grooming business because she wanted to combine art and working with animals. She makes sure that all the products she uses are safe, nontoxic, plant-based, and approved by the National Dog Groomers Association. Anaïs has even partnered with her local humane society to give some pooches needing a groom a little something extra to help them get adopted. To see her latest creations, check out her Instagram: @anais_hayden

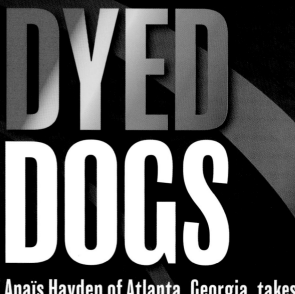

DOGS WITH JOBS

Alex Schulze trained his two Labradors to dive for lobsters.

In 2018, a Weimaraner puppy named Riley inspected artifacts and priceless objects at the Museum of Fine Arts in Boston, Massachusetts, to detect damaging pests (like beetles and moths).

In the 1880s, tax collector Karl Friedrich Louis Dobermann of Apolda, Germany, developed a breed of dog to help him collect taxes.

The University of Washington uses Conservation Canines to sniff for whale poop out at sea.

Beagles Candie and Chipper, part of the U.S. Customs and Border Protection's "Beagle Brigade," sniffed out two giant African snails in a passenger's luggage in Atlanta, Georgia!

The dog that played Toto in *The Wizard of Oz* was paid $125 a week—more than some of the actors on the set.

TWO FREEDOMS

Each year, Panama celebrates two independence days—the first on November 3, to mark its independence from Colombia in 1903, and the second on November 28, to commemorate its separation from Spain in 1821.

METALLIC TREE

Pycnandra acuminata, a rare tree native to forests on the South Pacific archipelago of New Caledonia, is able to collect large quantities of nickel from the ground. The tree has evolved to suck heavy metals out of the soil and store them in its stems and leaves—and its blue-green sap contains up to 25 percent nickel.

$58,000 DINNER

A Dubai tourist and seven friends ran up a bill of $58,000 for a 20-course dinner at Maggie's Restaurant in Shanghai, China. Owner and chef Sun Zhaoguo specially sourced and prepared the dishes, which included crocodile tail soup ($2,449) and abalone with sake jelly ($1,886). The service fee was $5,542.

BLUE HAZE

The Blue Mountains in New South Wales, Australia, get their name from the color of the fine haze that often hangs over them. The haze is made of oil emitted in large quantities from the abundant eucalyptus trees that grow there.

SACRED ROCK

The sacred Australian rock Uluru, also known as Ayers Rock, stands 1,141 ft (348 m) above the surrounding desert at its highest point, but it is believed to stretch for another 1.6 mi (2.5 km) underground.

HUGE ROUNDABOUT

A traffic roundabout at Putrajaya, Malaysia, is 2.2 mi (3.5 km) in diameter and encircles an area that can easily fit 100 football fields.

154 CHEESES

Johnny Di Francesco, chef at 400 Gradi restaurant in Melbourne, Australia, created a pizza topped with 154 varieties of cheese.

The eruption of Hawaii's Mount Kilauea in 2018 poured so much molten lava into Green Lake, the largest freshwater lake on the Big Island, that it completely boiled away.

Desert Dive

Lake Karum is visible through a hole in the salt flat of the Danakil Depression in Ethiopia! At Lake Karum, you can walk on water. Well, on the thick salt that covers the water, at least. Karum is one of two crystal-clear salt lakes on the northern end of the Danakil Depression, a vast salt flat measuring 155 mi (250 km) long and up to 44 mi (70 km) wide. It remains a testament to another time when the area was completely submerged by saline water. The salt is hundreds of feet deep in some places, but a hole in the crust allows tourists to enjoy a saltwater soak.

URBAN WATERFALL

This astounding Chinese skyscraper incorporates a breathtaking 354-ft-tall (108-m) waterfall into its façade.

The Liebian International Building in Guiyang, southwest China, measures nearly 397 ft (121 m) tall. A modest height in comparison to other skyscrapers like the Empire State Building, which stands at 1,454 ft (443 m) tall, the Chinese skyscraper is renowned for an entirely different design element: it boasts one of the largest artificial waterfalls in the world. Fed by four underground tanks filled with rainwater, its architectural team has successfully transported a little nature into the heart of the urban landscape.

ADRENALINE RUSH

Christopher Horsley, from Lancashire, England, abseiled down into three active volcanoes on the Pacific islands of Vanuatu that were filled with red-hot, molten 1,292°F (700°C) lava and, on returning to the top, performed a daring handstand on the edge of one volcano.

The purpose of this camping trip to the active lava lake of Marum was to access the crater floor to capture drone photography. Horsley and his crew spent the night at the bottom of the basin, making it a world first. Descending to the crater floor takes Horsley more than two hours—and another two to come back up. He has made a total of 14 descents into Marum.

HOT STUFF!
CLOSE ENCOUNTERS WITH ACTIVE VOLCANOES!

Q: HOW WOULD YOU DESCRIBE WHAT YOU DO?

A: I'm an extremophile and an activist. I'm a volcano access specialist and adventure photographer.

Q: HOW DID YOU BECOME AN ADVENTURE PHOTOGRAPHER?

A: Through a passion for the remote and tribal culture, I was drawn to the lens as my primary view for documenting such cultures and observing the similarities between our worlds. I feel humbled by my journey into photography; it was a road, not a decision.

Q: YOUR MAIN FOCUS IS EXPEDITIONS. WERE YOU ALWAYS DRAWN TO NATURE?

A: I'm drawn to the extremes of this planet—volcanoes—and the people who surround them. I think the draw to volcanoes is because of their ability to be so destructive and brutal, yet provide so much for our planet's construction and lives that thrive on volcanic riches.

Q: WHAT IS THE MOST MESMERIZING SIGHT FOR YOU AROUND THE GLOBE?

A: Staring into the depths of a lava lake as molten rock explodes to the surface of the earth meters below your feet—that's pretty awesome!

Q: HOW DO YOU PREPARE FOR EXPEDITIONS?

A: Getting a good knowledge of locations, weather conditions, cultures, and topics of interest in the area is key. But I mainly prepare by eating as healthy and fresh as possible, since long expeditions usually mean no fresh produce.

RED HOT LAVA!

1,292°F (700°C)

DARING HANDSTAND ON THE EDGE!

Q: HOW DO YOU FEEL WHEN STANDING NEXT TO A LAVA LAKE?

A: When you are down on the crater floor, the sound of the lava lake is projected by the crater walls, and there is some kind of infra-sound that you feel through your whole body as the magma surges at the surface. It's a feeling that resonates how inferior you are to this mass of energy.

DO YOU HAVE ANY FUTURE EXPEDITION PLANS?

A: Tribes, volcanoes, extreme weather—anything that could kill me, really.

Murderer Shoes

It is believed that shamans from Australia's aborigines wore these shoes (made of emu bird feathers and human hair, all matted together with human blood) when called upon to execute a person guilty of murder. It was believed that these shoes would leave no tracks, ensuring a clean getaway. Also called *kurdaitcha* shoes.

Valentine's Day Massacre Brick

Brick from the execution wall of the St. Valentine's Day Massacre (February 14, 1929), during the Chicago gangland war.

THIS IS AN ACTUAL BRICK FROM CHICAGO'S ST. VALENTINE'S DAY MASSACRE WALL OF FEBRUARY 14, 1929 AT 2122 N. CLARK STREET

Escape rope which was hidden in this bottle under ground until the inmate used it.

Ripley's Exhibit

Cat. No. 15365

Prison Escape Rope

Hidden in a bottle and buried in the dirt floor of a cell in Washington State Prison, this rope was kept by a prisoner to be used during an escape attempt.

inside the vault

Droid Dome

The Star Wars franchise has inspired many nerdy acts of excessive fandom, but none hold a candle to one observatory in Germany painted to look like R2-D2. Professor Hubert Zitt, from the German university Hochschule Kaiserslautern, decided on the sci-fi paint job after noticing the observatory's shape perfectly matched this mischievous robot. No word on when C-3PO will stop in for a visit.

Quantum Canvas

From Van Gogh's *The Starry Night* to da Vinci's *Mona Lisa*, these micro-copies of famous artwork measure no larger than the width of a human hair. Scientists at the University of Queensland stumbled upon the imaging method while researching the microscopic quantum world. Using a laser to create a "light stamp," they forge these images on quantum blobs of matter known as Bose–Einstein condensates. Now that's a hairy situation!

AS SMALL AS A HUMAN HAIR

FOOD CANS
Delivery company DoorDash used 6,853 cans of food to create a giant mosaic image of an African elephant on Santa Monica Pier, California.

CUNNING DISGUISES
Twentieth-century German artist George Grosz was a master of disguise who liked to dress up as a cowboy, a Dutch businessman, and even his own butler.

LAST STATUE
Leonardo da Vinci's last statue—a 24-ft-high (7.6-m) bronze sculpture of a horse—took more than 500 years to complete. He started working on it in 1482, but war with France meant that bronze was needed for military cannons instead; then in 1519, da Vinci died. In 1994, Italian sculptor Nina Akamu brought da Vinci's plans and drawings to life, and five years later the 15-ton sculpture was unveiled in Milan.

TOTO LOOP
Max Siedentopf, a German-Namibian artist, set up a sound installation that uses solar power to play Toto's "Africa" on an endless loop in the Namib Desert.

SAND SANTA
Sand artist Sudarsan Pattnaik spent two days creating a 30-ft-tall (9-m) sculpture of Santa Claus from sand and 10,000 plastic bottles in Odisha, India.

NOOD SCULPTURES

Artist Serghei Pakhomoff never got the "Don't play with your food!" lesson as a kid, because his intricate works of art are crafted solely from pasta.

Pakhomoff's masterpieces include miniature models of boats, planes, cars, and even towns. He painstakingly assembles them out of various types of pasta from spaghetti, to penne, to linguine, to lasagna noodles. Each creation, from the linguine truck to the macaroni motorbike, takes Pakhomoff between 20 and 30 hours to complete. His most challenging model to date? A car, complete with reclining seats, mirrors, and doors that open!

CAREER SWITCH
Before codesigning the Barbie doll, Jack Ryan had been an engineer working on guided missile systems.

BEATLES CONNECTION
Actress Jane Asher was Paul McCartney's girlfriend between 1963 and 1968—and 20 years earlier her mother, Margaret, had taught the oboe to future Beatles producer George Martin.

CAR CHASE
The Intercept was a popular Russian TV game show from the 1990s where, in order to win a car, the contestant had to "steal" it and avoid being captured by the police for 35 minutes. The car chase took place through real Moscow streets, where traffic laws had to be obeyed. The aim of the show, which attracted millions of viewers per episode, was to discourage car thieves since the contestant usually got caught.

BODY JUDGE
Arthur Conan Doyle, creator of Sherlock Holmes, was a judge at one of the world's first body-building competitions, held on September 14, 1901, in London, England.

CAT MIMIC
Once while bored during a rehearsal, Wolfgang Amadeus Mozart began imitating a cat by leaping on tables and chairs, meowing, and doing somersaults.

BOATS ICE SKATING ACROSS THE FROZEN LAKE!

METAL SKATES

ICE SAILING

Racing across a frozen lake at more than 40 mph (64 kmph), ice sailing involves riding on a 12-ft-long (3.7-m) boat with metal skates and a large sail.

Ice sailing isn't for the faint of heart. Nevertheless, it continues to bring a devoted following to places like Lake Champlain, the 13th largest lake in the United States. Sitting on the border between upstate New York and Vermont and just 12 mi (19 km) from the Canadian border, Champlain sees plenty of winter ice. This is drawing adrenaline junkies from across the country, looking to fly across the lake's surface at breakneck speeds.

BREAKOUT III

Ice sailing has been a mode of transportation and a source of winter fun for hundreds of years!

FAN FEED

Unintended Message

A fire department in Start, Louisiana, is known as the Start Fire Department, and their emblem is a bushel of flaming cotton! As Louisianan Richard Gibson tells Ripley's, the aptly named fire department organized in 1987. They commemorated their 25th anniversary in 2012, despite a name that leaves just about everybody shaking their heads.

BABY NAMES
Beau Jessup, a teen from Gloucestershire, England, paid her way through college by devising an online service that helps Chinese parents choose a suitable English name for their babies. In three and a half years, she helped name 677,900 Chinese babies.

MISSING BOOKS
Vera Walker, of Orlando, Florida, ordered a set of Dr. Seuss books for her four-year-old granddaughter in 1998—but by the time the post office finally delivered them in 2018, her granddaughter was an adult with a five-year-old son of her own! The post office said the package had been stuck inside an old mailbox for 20 years.

THIRSTY SURVIVOR
Brooke Phillips survived for six days in the Australian outback 1,700 mi (2,700 km) east of Perth in baking temperatures of 95°F (35°C) by drinking the windshield wiper fluid from her car and also her own urine.

SAME CARD
Ken Myers, from Leeds, England, has sent his wife Valerie the same Valentine's Day card for more than 40 years, but with a new coded message inside each year.

TIME CAPSULE
Construction crews demolishing the former Swampscott Middle School, Massachusetts, in 2018 found a 124-year-old time capsule buried beneath the building. Dated April 28, 1894, it contained two newspapers from the time, remnants of military uniforms from the Civil War, a war medal, and the names of local people who served in the war.

LOST FINGERS
Andrew Shilliday, a champion bagpipe player from Dungannon, Northern Ireland, had all his fingers and thumbs amputated after a terrifying autoimmune disease turned them black with gangrene—but he has had a special bagpipe made so that he can play without fingers.

CROC TERROR
When Shantelle Johnson and Colen Nulgit's car became stuck in a crocodile-infested swamp in Australia's Keep River National Park, they were rescued after writing HELP in giant letters in the mud. Terrified of the massive reptiles, they stayed in their car all night, but then the tide rose, forcing them to abandon the vehicle. Luckily, rescuers flying overhead spotted their makeshift sign and hauled them to safety after the 24-hour ordeal.

ANIMAL CANNIBALS

Although some insects and arachnids develop a fatal taste for their mates, it turns out baby earwigs often eat their siblings!

When snakes get angry from hunger, all bets are off, which means not only will they eat other snakes, but they sometimes even go after their own tails, accidentally eating themselves like the ancient *ouroboros* symbol.

Tiger salamanders not only happily eat one another, but some even morph during their larval stage, developing a broader head and more prominent teeth to eat their kin with.

In July 2019, terrifying footage emerged of a cannibalistic Great White shark nearly biting a 12-ft-long (3.7-m) rival in two, and recent fossil finds further confirm that sharks have been eating each other for at least 300 million years!

Scientists in western Poland made a grisly discovery in July 2013 while inspecting an abandoned nuclear bunker—nearly a million wood ants trapped inside and surviving on the bodies of their deceased!

Under the right circumstances, chickens take their "pecking order" to the next level, resulting in outbreaks of cannibalism that, if left unchecked, can spread rapidly through whole flocks.

Tasty Toad

Food artist Sarah Hardy creates chocolate creatures that are so realistic they look as if they could run, fly, or, in the case of this toad, hop away. The mother of two lives in the UK and also enjoys crafting chocolate into marine life, invertebrates, and anatomically correct human organs. While her sweet treats might not look very appetizing, we think Willy Wonka would approve!

RATTLER ATTACK

Todd, a six-month-old golden retriever, bravely jumped in front of owner Paula Godwin to save her from a rattlesnake bite while she was hiking near her home in Anthem, Arizona. The snake bit Todd in the face, but he was given antivenom at an animal hospital and recovered.

FIRST ADVENTURE

The first time she ever went outdoors, Lily, an 18-month-old cat owned by Ruca Abbott of Steveston, British Columbia, Canada, crawled into the bumper of a neighbor's car and went on a 54-mi (86-km) joyride, which only ended when the driver saw the cat's tail sticking out from under the car.

FIRE RESCUE

Larry Moore was saved from a house fire in Hutchinson, Kansas, thanks to his alert dog, Lucifer. Moore was asleep in a living room chair when Lucifer jumped onto his lap and woke him up. It was only then that he realized the house was on fire.

WAKE-UP CALL

A man was asleep in his Pulaski, New York, apartment when a 6-ft-long (1.8-m) red-tailed boa constrictor fell through his bedroom ceiling and landed on him. The snake had escaped from its enclosure in the apartment above.

INFLATING EEL

To scoop up larger prey than it can usually eat with its small teeth, the gulper eel (*Eurypharynx pelecanoides*) inflates its mouth to several times its normal size so that it looks like a black balloon. After feeding, it deflates and swims away.

STINGS HIMSELF

Once a month for more than 10 years, Pepe Casanas, a 78-year-old Cuban farmer, has hunted down a blue scorpion to sting himself with, because he believes its venom eases his rheumatic pain. He places the scorpion on the part of his body where he feels most pain and squeezes the insect until it stings him. He says that after the initial sting, the pain goes away.

BUBBLE BUGS

Photographer Carrot Lim Choo How has captured incredible, close-up images of bubble-blowing wasps, and you won't believe your eyes!

How captured the images while photographing a wasp nest in a factory compound in Kedah, Malaysia. The photos show wasps with perfectly spherical droplets of water extending from their mouths, similar to chewing-gum bubbles. And there's a surprising scientific explanation for the whole thing. To clean excess moisture from the nest, the wasps vacuum it up and then expel it outside in the form of water drops.

CAR SPINNERS

Car spinning has emerged out of South Africa's criminal underworld in recent years as a legitimate sport where men and women vie for top honors and popped tires.

Welcome to the world of South African spinning. Drivers compete in three-minute-long sets involving plenty of nausea-inducing spins, daredevil stunts (both in and out of the car), and exploding tires. The tricks appear both death- and physics-defying, from suicide slides to crazy flips. Because of the sport's illicit origins, few rules exist and courage, audacity, and bravado win the day.

PERSONAL PALACE

Businessman Do Van Thien has built a vast, European-style palace in the rural Gia Vien region of Vietnam. Thanh Thang Palace (named after his two sons) has cost him $17 million, using 1,000 tons of iron, 5,000 tons of cement, and tens of thousands of bricks. The six-story-high building covers an area of 18,298 sq ft (1,700 sq m) and features underground garages that can accommodate 50 cars.

FACE SLAPPING

As part of the 2019 Siberian Power Show, the Russian city of Krasnoyarsk hosted a face-slapping championship, where people took turns to slap each other across the face with the palm of their hand until one was knocked out. If both were left standing after three slaps apiece, judges decided the winner based on power and technique. The champion, Vasiliy Kamotskiy, received a prize of almost $470.

LUXURY CAR

A one-off luxury Bugatti sports car (*La Voiture Noire* ["The Black Car"]) sold for $18.9 million in Geneva, Switzerland, in 2019.

1,000

The number of streetlights that illuminate a 1.8-mi (3-km) stretch of road in the Chinese village of Taojia. Streetlights are usually placed around 160 ft (50 m) apart, but these are only 10 ft (3 m) from each other, even though there are often no cars on the narrow road for hours.

NUMBER 11

The Swiss town of Solothurn has a fixation with the number 11. There are 11 churches and chapels in the town, 11 historical fountains, 11 museums, 11 towers, and the clock in the town square features an 11-hour dial with the number 12 missing. The town's Cathedral of St. Ursus, which took 11 years to build, has 11 doors, 11 bells, and 11 altars, and the outer staircase comprises three sets of 11 steps. The local beer is called Oufi (11 in the regional dialect). The obsession with 11 is said to have been inspired by an ancient folk legend and dates back to at least 1252, when the town council was elected with 11 members.

CURIOSITY SHOP

Curiosities from the 5th Corner, a shop and museum owned by Henry Scragg in Essex, England, sells old human and animal skulls. Among the hundreds of weird items on display are tribal skulls, a human fetus in a jar, a human hand with a tumor, a child's prosthetic arm from the 1940s, animal hair in glass bottles, a woman's ovaries preserved in a jar of formaldehyde, and a human skull cap that has been made into a decorative bowl.

THE LAST STRAW

To raise awareness about plastic pollution and the dangers facing our oceans today, an artist crafted an 11-ft (3.4-m) wave using 168,000 plastic straws.

By 2050, there will be more plastic in the ocean than fish, and artist Benjamin Von Wong wanted to bring this stark reality to life through visual art. But contributing to the problem by purchasing fresh straws for his aptly titled art installation *Strawpocalypse* was out of the question. Instead, he worked tirelessly with Zero Waste Saigon, Starbucks Vietnam, and hundreds of volunteers over the course of six months to collect, wash, and sort the 168,000 straws required for the upcycle masterpiece.

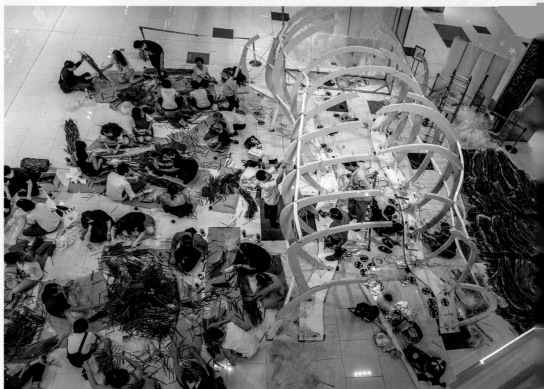

Raincircle

Rainbows are full circles rather than arcs, which means you can stop looking for gold at their "ends." Rainbows need just two ingredients: sunlight and raindrops. But to see them requires near-perfect conditions. You must face away from the sun (180°) and then look away from this point at a 42° angle. This allows you to see about one-fourth of the visible sky and a rainbow in the form of an arc. But what you see gets obstructed by the ground. Viewed from the atmosphere, without the limitations of the horizon, rainbows are actually shaped like full circles.

LUCKY ESCAPE
A two-year-old girl from Changzhou, China, survived with only minor injuries after falling from the 17th floor of an apartment building. Trees cushioned her 200-ft (60-m) fall, and when she did hit the ground, it had been softened by recent rainfall.

SHOP PRIZE
Dutch sci-fi fan Ceisjan Van Heerdan won a Welsh bookshop in a prize draw. The store owner, Paul Morris, was retiring and gave his customers at Bookends in Cardigan the chance to win the shop and its contents if they spent more than $30.

BIG PROPOSAL
Bob Lempa proposed to his girlfriend Peggy Baker by writing MARRY ME in 45-ft-tall (14-m), 31-ft-wide (9.5-m) letters in the snowy grass of Maggie Daley Park in Chicago. He needed to write the message in giant letters so that she could see it from the 37th floor of a nearby building where she worked.

SUNDANCE KID
Harry Longabaugh became known as the Sundance Kid because he served a jail term for stealing a horse from a ranch in Sundance, Wyoming, in 1887.

WEDDING DRESS
After bridesmaid Grayleigh Oppermann forgot to pack her dress when traveling from Houston, Texas, to Costa Rica for her sister's wedding, Southwest Airlines saved the day by delivering the dress for free on a last-minute flight.

BIRTHDAY GREETINGS
After Chris Ferry's sons rented a billboard near Linwood, New Jersey, plastered with his phone number and a request for people to send him birthday wishes, he received more than 15,000 calls and texts from strangers all over the world.

Alex Chu, a 19-year-old lacrosse goalie at Wheaton College, Massachusetts, was forced to sit on the bench for games in 2019 because he was unable to find a helmet that fit his wide head.

PIZZA POCKET
Mike Hourani, of Medford, New Jersey, has designed a hoodie with a special compartment to keep pizza warm. His "Pizza Pocket" hoodie has a zipper pocket that contains a washable, insulated pouch large enough to hold a slice of pizza.

SWEAT BEES
Doctors at Fooyin University Hospital in Taiwan found four sweat bees living in a woman's eye and feeding off the salt in her tears. She had been pulling weeds when the insects flew into her eye and became embedded in the socket.

WEDDING RING
Paula Stanton was reunited with her diamond-encrusted wedding ring nine years after accidentally flushing it down the toilet of her home in Somers Point, New Jersey. The missing ring was found in a nearby sewer.

PROFESSIONAL ARGUER
At Chinese online marketplace Taobao, people can hire a stranger to argue on their behalf with companies or individuals. An angry phone call or text costs $3, but the fee for these professional quarrelers rises for longer arguments.

POTTER WEDDING
Allison and Steven Price had a Harry Potter–themed wedding in Buckinghamshire, England, and held it on July 31—the birthday of both Harry Potter and author J. K. Rowling. Allison said she fell for her future husband partly because he looked like Ron Weasley.

TIMELY FIND
On April 3, 2019, Joseph and Karen Moore, from St. Peters, Missouri, found a $50,000 winning lottery ticket in the glove compartment of their car—just one day before the expiration date.

RUNNING
OF THE REXES

On July 7, 2019, spectators at Auburn, Washington's Emerald Downs did a double take as more than 20 people in *Tyrannosaurus rex* costumes participated in a race of Jurassic proportions.

Although the identities of the racers have yet to be revealed, Tom Harris, Emerald Down's announcer, did give shout-outs to runners including Dino Dasher, Rex Girlfriend, and Ramblin' Rex. But it was Regular Unleaded who dashed to first place at the finish line. Videos of the race have since gone viral, with internet commentators enthusiastically embracing the first "Dino Derby" of its kind.

READY, SET, GO!

EMERALD DOWNS

7   6   5   4   3   2   1

Chopper Cinema

After impulse buying a decommissioned army helicopter, Maria Merry of Chippenham, England, transformed it into a one-of-a-kind home theater. An avid fan of aviation, Maria had the huge chopper airlifted to her home and placed in the garage. Thousands of dollars in upgrades later, she and her son pile into the helicopter whenever they want to enjoy a movie. From custom sound effects to a candy dispenser, secret minibar, smoke machine, and sofa bed, who would've guessed a retired army aircraft could be so comfortable?

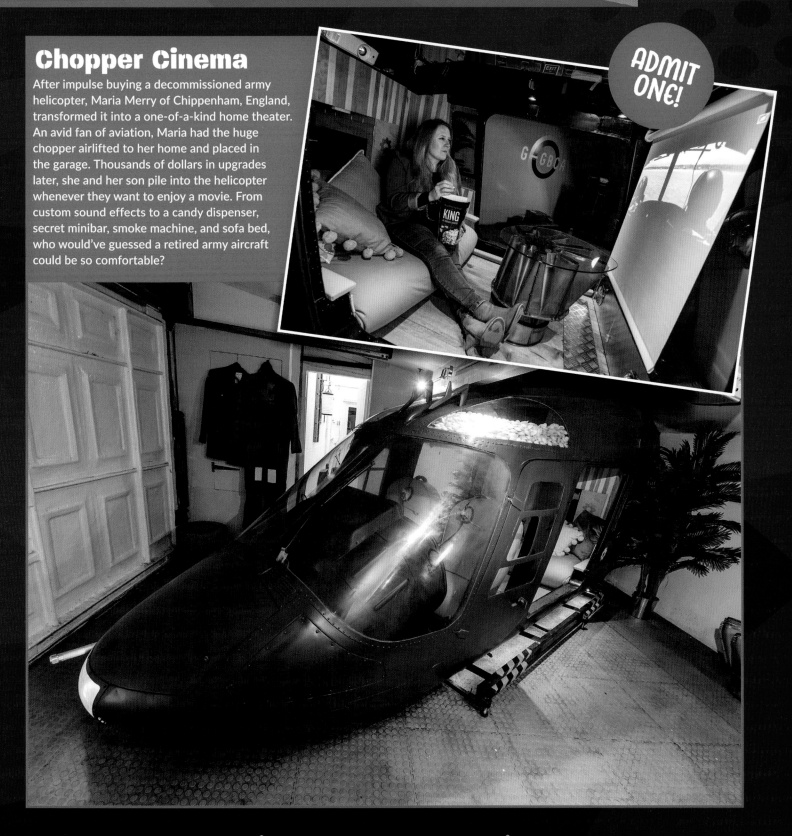

ADMIT ONE!

OLD SCHOOL

The school that served as Hill Valley High School in the movie *Back to the Future* was Whittier High, California—Richard Nixon's school from 1928–1930.

SECRET SHREDDER

UK street artist Banksy built a secret, remote-controlled shredder into the frame of his painting *Girl With Balloon* so that it self-destructed moments after it was sold at auction in 2018 for over $1.3 million.

Some parents in the United States claim their children are starting to speak in a British accent after watching the TV show *Peppa Pig.*

PARKER HOME

The New York City house that Peter Parker (Spider-Man) grew up in is 20 Ingram Street in Forest Hills, Queens. This is a real address and from 1974 onward was home to a family named Parker! Also, Spider-Man's archenemy is the Green Goblin (real name Norman Osborn), and from 1979 onward, Andrew and Suzanne Parker's neighbor in Queens was Terri Osborne. The families were both living there when the *Spider-Man* movie was released in 2002.

Hive-Thru

To support bee conservation, McDonald's created a tiny restaurant for bees that's a working hive complete with a drive-thru, iconic Golden Arches, and plenty of honeycombs. Starting with a single store in Sweden adding a beehive to its roof, four stores quickly followed suit, and even more are committed to relandscaping their facilities with bee-friendly habitats. Soon, McDonald's Sweden took it to the next level by creating a fully functioning McHive. It sold at auction for $10,000, with proceeds going to Ronald McDonald House charities.

"ONE MCPOLLEN, PLEASE!"

Radar Love

A recent ladybug swarm proved so massive it was caught on radar! On June 4, 2019, National Weather Service meteorologists first spotted the puzzling green blob on their radar screens. They scrambled to figure out what the formation could be since no impending rainstorms loomed. But a weather spotter in the vicinity soon reported it as a massive ladybug "bloom."

BROTHERLY LOVE
An escaped baby Maximilian parrot, native to the Amazon, called Sausage Rowles, was coaxed down from a tree in Devon, England, with a cell phone recording of her twin brother. Sausage's owner, Michelle Chubb, played the squawks of six-month-old Chico to entice Sausage to safety. Sausage takes his name from Michelle's partner, Adam Rowles.

DNA TEST
PooPrints is a service that uses DNA testing to identify dogs whose owners have failed to remove their poop from public places.

LONG EARS
The long-eared jerboa—a nocturnal, mouse-like rodent from Asia—has ears that are one-third longer than its head.

BAT BUILDING
Sugar Hall, a classroom building at the University of Louisiana at Monroe, was temporarily closed in January 2019 after it became infested with thousands of bats.

UNEXPECTED GIFT
In November 2018, a live albino boa constrictor was found in a bin of Goodwill donations in Fort Worth, Texas.

EXTRA EYE

In 2019, wildlife officials in Australia's Northern Territory found an unusual juvenile carpet python with three functioning eyes.

The snake had an eye on either side of its head and a third eye near the center of its skull. Rangers with the Northern Territory Parks and Wildlife Commission named the nearly 16-in-long (40-cm) python Monty. Unfortunately, the deformity made it difficult for the snake to eat, and it passed away at about four months old.

CODED COWS
Stray cows in Uttar Pradesh, India, are barcoded so that they can be tracked and stopped from destroying crops and blocking traffic.

LARGE LITTER
Cleo the Great Dane gave birth to 19 puppies at the Kingman Animal Hospital in Arizona. It took 11 staff members to assist in the multiple birth. Great Danes usually have litters of around eight puppies.

SEAL SQUATTERS
During the 2019 U.S. government shutdown, a colony of 100 elephant seals took over an unstaffed beach and car park at Drakes Beach, California.

TOP CAT
Wojciech Jabczynski climbed to the summit of Poland's 8,200-ft-high (2,500-m) Rysy Mountain and found a ginger domestic cat chilling out there!

DESERT ADVENTURE
Gaspar, a two-year-old dachshund owned by Janis Cavieres, survived for six days in Chile's Atacama Desert after escaping from an airplane. The dog had been traveling in a cage in the cargo hold, but after the plane had landed, the pet carrier fell onto the runway and opened on impact, prompting him to flee into the nearby desert. When Gaspar was finally caught, he had lost a lot of his body weight but soon made a full recovery.

Ripley's Exhibit
Cat. No. 6089

Stamp Painting: Hyacinths

Painting of purple and
pink hyacinth flowers
made out of postage stamps.
Created by Lore Collins.

Ripley's Exhibit
Cat. No. 9562

Devil Faced Fish

The underside of a dried
clearnose skate. This "devil
fish" is complete with
ghostly eyes, bat-like wings,
and a barbed tail. Also known
as "Jenny Hanivers," they
were presented as demon
spawn in the 16th century.

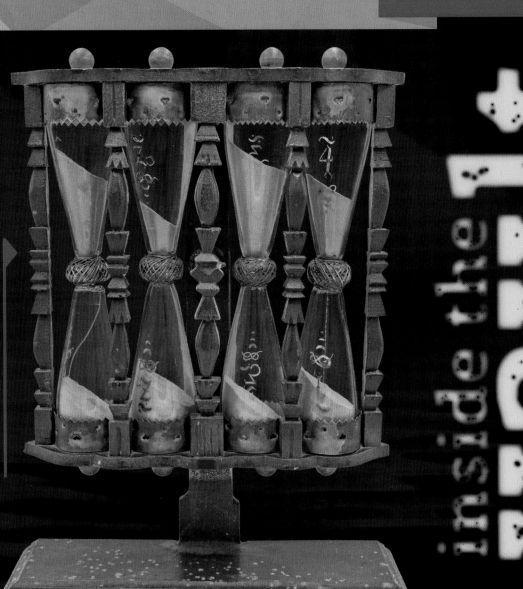

Ripley's Exhibit

Cat. No. 6953

Sand Clock

An 8th-century invention: the sand clock, or "hour glass." This four-glass version was collected by Ripley in Italy and marks the quarter, the half, the three-quarter, and the full hour.

inside the vault

Ripley's Exhibit

Cat. No. 9416

Chinese Root Carving

Chinese root carving of a Garuda sculpted from the contorted roots of a cherry tree. Acquired by Robert Ripley during his third visit to the Asian continent in 1937, this carving decorated Ripley's 10-room New York City Asian-inspired apartment.

KILLER CAKES

Baker Tanya Nisa, from Lincoln, England, bakes morbid cakes that closely resemble human body parts!

Her creations include a Victoria sponge in the design of amputated fingers and a Madeira cake in the shape of a severed head. Tanya's desserts can take anywhere from a few hours to a few days to finish, depending on the intricacy of her design. A set of fingers, for example, involves delicate painting with a fine-tipped brush. Tanya was inspired by the movie *Hannibal*, and her incredible attention to detail can be attributed to the seven years she has spent perfecting her skills.

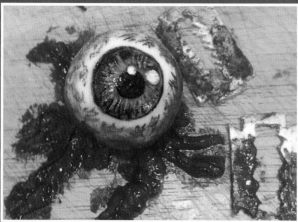

FAKE BLOOD!

FROZEN TRIBUTE

Residents of one Montreal, Canada, suburb reacted with shock and admiration when an approximately 20-ft-tall (6.1-m) real-life Olaf snowman inspired by Disney's *Frozen* popped up in their neighborhood.

It was constructed by YouTuber Benoit Sabourin, who logged more than 200 hours building it with the help of a "sketchy ladder."

On September 6, 2018, British musician Evelina De Lain played a piano concert at an altitude of 16,227 ft (4,946 m) at Singge La Pass in the Himalayas in sub-zero temperatures.

CRAZY CLOTHES
Swedish band Abba's stage costumes in the 1970s were deliberately garish and outrageous because the cost of clothes was tax deductible in Sweden if it could be proved that they were unsuitable for everyday wear.

GAMBLING DEBTS
Russian author Fyodor Dostoyevsky wrote his 1866 novel *The Gambler* in only 26 days to clear his gambling debts and meet a publisher's deadline. If the novel was turned in late, the publisher would have acquired for free the rights to everything Dostoyevsky wrote for the next nine years.

BODY QUOTES
Tattoo artist Monty Richthofen (aka Maison Hefner), from London, England, runs a project called "My Words, Your Body," where clients allow him to ink motivational quotes of his choice onto their body. They have no idea what the tattoo will say—they only decide where it goes on their body.

GIANT CARICATURE
Dean Foster, a South African–born artist based in Innisfail, Alberta, Canada, used an All-Terrain Vehicle and spray paint to create a 427 × 328 ft (130 × 100 m) caricature of two Canadian radio station DJs—CJAY 92's Jesse and JD—on a farm pasture.

CAMPAIGN SONG
Iraqi dictator Saddam Hussein used an Arabic version of Whitney Houston's "I Will Always Love You" as his reelection campaign song in 2002.

WHITE DIET
French composer Erik Satie only ever ate white food—eggs, sugar, grated bones, veal, animal fat, coconuts, chicken, rice, turnips, and white cheese. It's said that he once ate 150 oysters in a single sitting.

DREAM BOOKS
The idea for the *Twilight* books came to author Stephenie Meyer in a vivid dream on the night of June 2, 2003.

NAME CLASH
SpongeBob (SquarePants) was originally called SpongeBoy, but that name was trademarked by a brand of mop.

TIGHT BUDGET
The 1975 movie *Monty Python and the Holy Grail* was shot on a tight budget, and filming frequently had to stop when the castle, a plywood cutout, kept falling over in the wind. The running joke of the knights riding invisible horses and clapping coconut halves together to provide the sound of the hooves came about because the Pythons could not afford real horses.

GHOST SHIP
Artist Jason Stieva, from Whitby, Ontario, Canada, spent 14 months building a huge sculpture of a ghost pirate ship. *Leviathan—Ark of Apocalypse* weighs 200 lb (90 kg), measures 8 ft (2.4 m) tall and 7.5 ft (2.3 m) long, and contains hundreds of individual skeleton sculptures.

PIG MUSEUM

Stuttgart, Germany, boasts the largest pig museum in the world, featuring more than 42,000 different swine artifacts.

A former hog slaughterhouse, the Schweine Museum has turned over a new leaf with 25 rooms filled with piggy artifacts. From pink stuffed pig pyramids to the nostalgia of the piggy bank room and the bling of a massive rotating, golden boar, there's plenty of swine for everyone. Once guests have worked up a serious appetite, they can chow down at the museum's restaurant, where all things pork get served daily.

LUXURY SPUD!

Potato Hotel

Recycled from the Idaho Potato Commission's Big Idaho Potato Tour, this spud has hopped off the tour circuit and is now available for luxury lodging! Resting on 400 acres of Idaho farmland, the Idaho Potato Hotel is a stylish and cozy one bedroom, one bathroom retreat just outside of downtown Boise, Idaho. Former Big Idaho Potato Tour spokesperson Kristie Wolfe meticulously redesigned the potato to house a queen-sized bed, a mini fridge, an old record player, and plenty of electrical outlets.

FOSSIL BEER
The Lost Rhino Brewing Company of Virginia created Bone Dusters Paleo Ale, a beer brewed from the yeast collected from 35-million-year-old whale fossils.

SECRET RIVERS
There are more than 20 subterranean rivers flowing beneath the streets of London, England.

TV FENCE
A house on the Vietnamese island of Hon Thom has a fence made entirely out of dozens of old TV sets.

HIGHEST COURT
The basketball court on the top floor of the U.S. Supreme Court Building in Washington, D.C., is known as "the highest court in the land."

LARGE STATE
If the state of Western Australia were a country, it would be the 10th largest country in the world. The whole of Germany could fit inside Western Australia.

FAKE AMBULANCES
Traffic in Moscow is so bad that wealthy Russians sometimes hire fake ambulances to beat the jams.

28,000
The number of wineries in Slovenia—meaning there is a winery for every 75 people in the country.

EDIBLE STATUE
In 2018, Linyi City, China, unveiled a 20-ft-tall (6-m) statue of a rooster whose body was made from red and green chili peppers with legs crafted out of corn cobs.

TIDY DAY
Every year Russia has a special day called Subbotnik, when residents volunteer to sweep and tidy city streets.

CRATER CITY
The city of Middlesboro, Kentucky, is built entirely inside a 3.7-mi-wide (5.9-km) meteorite crater.

ROMANTIC STAMP
Every Valentine's Day, thousands of cards from all over the world are sent to the Post Office in Lover, Wiltshire, England, to be stamped with the village name.

MORE MUSEUMS
There are more museums in the United States (more than 35,000) than there are branches of Starbucks and McDonald's combined.

FIRST CRIME
In 2018, the Scottish island of Gigha experienced its first crime in 20 years, rocking the small population of 160.

BIG THINGS SMALL TOWN

You can dream big in the small town of Casey, Illinois—it's home to six supersized monuments that hold the world records for largest item!

When some of Casey's local businesses began shutting down, carpenter Jim Bolin was heartbroken. Instead of watching his childhood town die off, Bolin crafted the World's Largest Wind Chimes to reel people in. In constructing his "largest items" and "big things," Bolin thinks of what would pair well with a local business and builds it—free of charge—to display at each location.

WORLD'S LARGEST ROCKING CHAIR

WORLD'S LARGEST WIND CHIME

WORLD'S LARGEST GOLF TEE

WORLD'S LARGEST MAILBOX

WORLD'S LARGEST PITCHFORK

WORLD'S LARGEST WOODEN SHOES

Snow Spikes

A feature of high-altitude glaciers, penitentes occur in the Dry Andes above 13,123 ft (4,000 m) and can reach up to 16 ft (4.8 m) tall. First described by Charles Darwin in 1839, scientists are still debating why and how these spectacular blades of ice form. A common sight in the mountainous regions between Argentina and Chile, penitentes usually form in clusters. They measure between 1.18 in (3 cm) and 6.5 ft (2 m), although formations 16 ft (4.8 m) tall have also been recorded.

Ice Tree

Move over, Elsa! For 58 years, one family in Indianapolis, Indiana, has created 35- to 75-ft-tall (10.7- to 22.8-m) frozen trees using food coloring and a garden hose. Since 1961, Janet Veal and her family have perfected the art of crafting massive, rainbow-colored frozen trees. Growing the perfect ice tree requires temperatures between 5 and 29°F (−15 and −2°C). After building a massive frame from scrap lumber, they line it with brush and tree limbs. Once the structure gets sprayed with layer upon layer of water and food coloring, it takes on a frigid life of its own, a glittering monument to DIY winter landscaping.

CARNIVAL OF YETIS

Each year, Yetis flood Ratevo, near the town of Berovo in eastern Macedonia, for an epic battle against evil.

Like Halloween, where ghoulish costumes and jack-o'-lanterns scare away spirits during the "witching hour," the Macedonian Carnival of Yetis involves dressing like monsters to expel the nefarious forces of winter. Temperatures in this mountainous region average between –4 and –22°F (–20 to –30°C) during the October festival, which means piling on plenty of furs. Creepy masks complete the look, resulting in creatures that could occupy more than a few branches of Bigfoot's family tree.

OUTHOUSE RACING

For 30 years, the World Championship Outhouse Races in Virginia City, Nevada, have brought competitors together in a sprint to the toilet-paper finish line.

The event started in the autumn of 1990 when Storey County put forth an ordinance to ban all outhouses. In response, residents of the quasi-ghost town took to the streets, bringing their outhouses with them. The odd assemblage inspired the creation of a latrine racing event like no other. Teams of three in full costume push, pedal, and drag their homemade outhouses down C Street, creating a quirky event with plenty of bathroom humor.

Bathtub Opera

On August 29, 2019, concertgoers arrived at the Lucerna building in Prague, Czech Republic, to climb into bathtubs installed on the roof. There, they listened to arias from Mozart's opera *Don Giovanni* performed by Adam Plachetka. Dressed in formal clothes, they braved the waters for the half-hour performance, sparkling wine in hand.

ROBOT ROBBER

Responding to reports of a possible home invasion after a house sitter called 911 in fear that someone was in the bathroom, police deputies in Beaverton, Oregon, rushed to the scene, opened the bathroom door with guns drawn, and found that the culprit was nothing more dangerous than a robotic, automatic vacuum cleaner.

BATHTUB ORDEAL

Alison Gibson was stuck in the bathtub of her home in Chesaning, Michigan, for five days before the alarm was raised by her mailman.

MISPLACED ANGER

In 2018, officials in Portland, Michigan, asked Facebook users to quit sending them angry messages about Portland, Oregon.

To win a $62,400 bet with fellow poker player Rory Young, Rich Alati spent 20 days in complete isolation and total darkness in a small bathroom in Las Vegas, Nevada.

PAINFUL LESSON

While attempting to steal gas by siphoning it from a truck outside a store in Portland, Oregon, a thief accidentally set his pants on fire.

VACATION PHOTOS

Scientists in New Zealand found a USB drive containing someone's vacation pictures inside a frozen slab of leopard seal poop.

PRAYERS ANSWERED

Two teen swimmers, Tyler Smith and Heather Brown, prayed for help after becoming stranded 2 mi (3.2 km) from shore off the coast of St. Augustine, Florida, when strong currents pulled them out to sea. They were eventually rescued by a boat called the *Amen*.

Poo Paint

To keep her Toyota Corolla cool when temperatures sizzle, Sejal Shah, from Ahmedabad, India, covers the exterior in cow dung. This practice provides just the right amount of stinky insulation. She got the idea from locals who use the dung paste on the floors and walls of mud houses to decrease summer heat, which can reach upward of 100°F (38°C).

STRANGE BUDDIES

Frogs living in South America face an endless stream of predators, from spiders to snakes and a variety of mammals.

This can make it downright dangerous to get a good night's sleep, unless you're a humming frog. Turns out, they've struck an unlikely bargain with Peruvian tarantulas. The tarantulas allow the amphibians to live in their burrows and even protect them from predators. So, what do the frogs do to earn their keep? They keep the tarantulas' burrows clear of unwanted parasites and ants that eat the spiders' eggs.

POLICE WARNING

A parrot was arrested in northern Brazil after it was discovered that he had been trained to warn his criminal owners about impending police raids by squawking, "Mama, police!" in Portuguese.

DEADLY DISCOVERY

After her dogs started barking at her pickup truck that was parked outside her home in Chonburi, Thailand, Chutikarn Kaewthongchaijaruen discovered a deadly 16-ft-long (4.9-m) king cobra lurking in the vehicle's engine compartment.

OCTOPUS SLAP

Kayaker Kyle Mulinder was paddling off the coast of New Zealand's South Island when he was slapped in the face with an octopus by a seal! He had, unfortunately, wandered into the middle of a fight between a large male seal and an octopus.

WELL CAMOUFLAGED

Measuring less than 1 in (2.4 cm) in size, Bargibant's pygmy seahorses are so tiny and so well camouflaged to resemble the coral on which they live that they remained undiscovered until 1969, when New Caledonian scientist Georges Bargibant took coral samples to his laboratory for study and noticed a pair of seahorses on them.

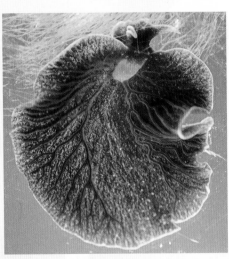

Solar-Powered Sea Slug

This solar-powered sea slug derives its superpowers from algae! According to scientists at Rutgers University–New Brunswick, a sea slug known as the *Elysia chlorotica* transforms into a solar-powered green machine. How? By sucking millions of jade-colored plastids from algae. These plastids not only give the slug an emerald tinge but also allow it to act as a plant, receiving sustenance directly from the rays of the sun.

FOOT-DIALED

After marine mammal veterinarian Dr. Claire Simeone received 10 silent phone calls in quick succession from her hospital on Hawaii's Big Island, she discovered that the culprit was a gecko that had crawled into the laboratory and was perched on a phone, making dozens of calls with his feet.

BARKING DRONES

To herd their sheep, some farmers in New Zealand use flying drones that bark like dogs. The drone has a feature that records sounds and then plays them over a loud speaker. A herding job that takes two hours using two people and two teams of dogs can be completed in only 45 minutes with a single drone.

LONG EMBRACE

During the mating season, Indian stick insects can remain coupled together in a tight embrace for up to 79 days. The male uses his legs to hold the female firmly in place.

COW DATING

Some farmers in England use a Tinder-inspired dating app to find potential partners for their cows. The cattle love app is called Tudder—a mix of Tinder and udder—and allows farmers to swipe right on animals they like the look of.

MOOVING ALONG

A couple in Hathaway, Louisiana, saved a five-legged calf suffering from polymelia from slaughter and even reunited it with its mother.

A rare birth defect, polymelia only affects less than four in every 100,000 cattle around the world. Despite the rarity of the condition, Matt Alexander and his fiancée Maghin Davis rescued a calf with a fifth leg atop its head. They were also able to purchase her mother and reunite the two. Alexander and Davis report that the calf, which they named Elsie, remains in excellent health and that there are no plans to have the extra leg surgically removed.

GREAT BLUE HOLE

The undersea Great Blue Hole off the coast of Belize measures 984 ft (300 m) across and 410 ft (125 m) deep.

At a depth of about 350 ft (106 m) inside the natural marine sinkhole the water has no oxygen, resulting in a conch "graveyard" created by thousands of shellfish that swam too deep and died. The hole was once on dry land but became submerged around 10,000 years ago.

BALANCING ROCK
Pivot Rock in Eureka Springs, Arkansas, balances precariously on a base more than 10 times smaller than its top.

HORROR SETTING
The iconic gas station located at the side of Highway 304 in Bastrop, Texas, which served as the setting for the 1974 horror movie *The Texas Chainsaw Massacre*, is now a restaurant with four cabins so that people can dine and sleep there.

MINIATURE EXCAVATION
For more than 14 years, Joe Murray has been slowly excavating the basement of his home in Shaunavon, Saskatchewan, Canada, with a fleet of radio-controlled miniature trucks, bulldozers, and diggers.

LINGUISTICALLY DIVERSE
More than 850 languages are spoken in Papua New Guinea. Although English is one of four official languages, it is only spoken by about 2 percent of the population.

FISH SHOWER
Hundreds of live fish rained down on cars and streets during a fierce storm in Malta on February 24, 2019. The fish—mostly sea bream—were blown ashore by a combination of gale force winds and rough seas.

FAMOUS FIRSTS
Seattle was one of the first American cities to put police officers on bicycles and the first to play Muzak in stores and offices.

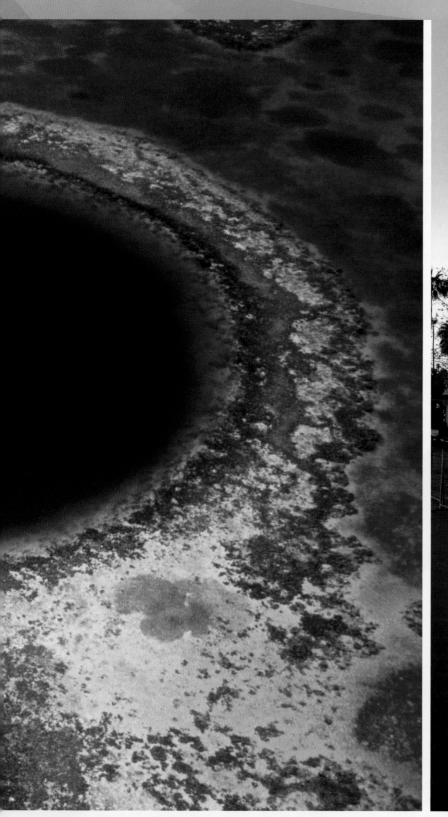

Tumbleweed Christmas Tree

Look, but don't touch! This Christmas tree in Chandler, Arizona, is built out of approximately 1,000 tumbleweeds. Collected from the outskirts of the city, these tumbleweeds are piled high onto a 25-ft-tall (7.6-m) wire frame, sprayed with 25 gal (95 l) of white paint, 20 gal (76 l) of flame retardant, and then sprinkled with 65 lb (29 kg) of glitter! A stunning 1,200 holiday lights adorn this festive fir. This holiday tradition goes back to 1957, and today it draws a crowd of about 12,000.

GENEROUS GESTURE
Although Steve's Pizza, in Battle Creek, Michigan, does not usually do takeouts, one of its managers, 18-year-old Dalton Shaffer, made and personally delivered two pizzas to Julie and Rich Morgan 225 mi (362 km) away in Indianapolis, Indiana—a seven-hour round trip. The couple had been fans of the restaurant when they lived in Battle Creek and had hoped to return there for Julie's 56th birthday, only for cancer patient Rich to be too ill to travel.

CONCH ISLAND
Conch Island is a manmade mountain in the British Virgin Islands that is made out of millions of conch shells discarded by fishermen over hundreds of years. The island is big enough to be visible on Google Earth.

HOT AND COLD
Temperatures in China's Turpan Depression can range from 118°F (48°C) in the summer to –20°F (–29°C) in the winter.

HOTTEST LAVA
An underwater volcano in the Pacific Ocean contains the hottest lava ever measured—a blistering 2,444°F (1,340°C).

COLOSSAL BERG
An iceberg the size of Lower Manhattan broke off from Greenland's Helheim Glacier in 2018. The colossal berg measured 4 mi (6.4 km) wide, was 0.5 mi (0.8 km) thick, and weighed 10 billion tons. It took about 30 minutes to separate.

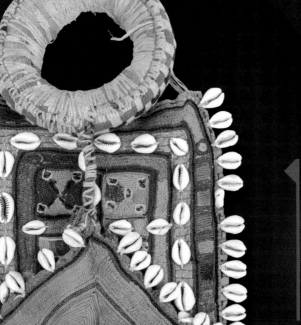

Indian Head Balancing Ring

Small ring used to balance items on human heads. The ring has two woven cloths attached and is ornamented with cowrie shells. Some women have been known to regularly transport goods on their heads at up to 70 percent of their body weight.

Egyptian Mummy Foot

Genuine Egyptian mummy's foot with linen still attached. From the former estate of a British doctor, in England.

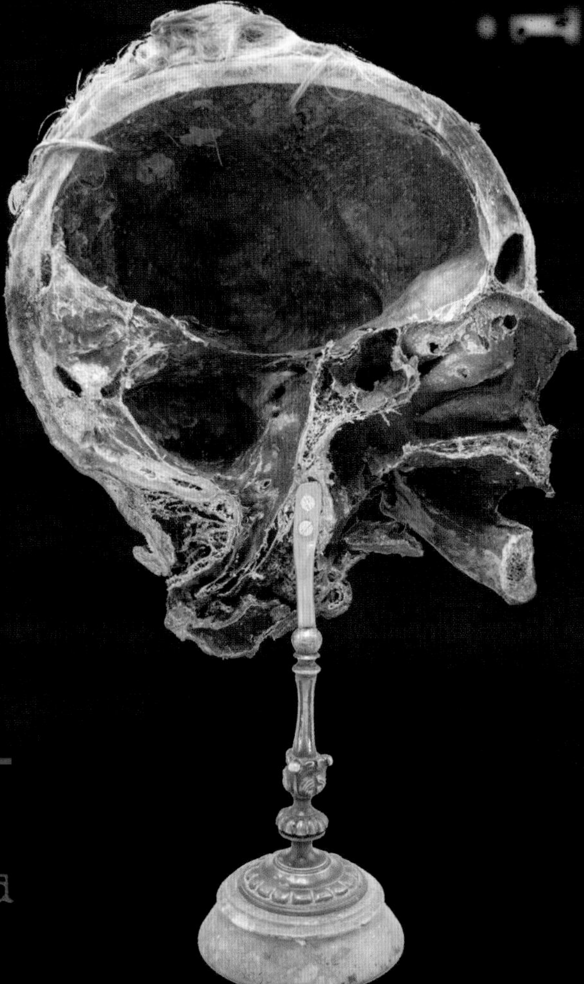

Ripley's Exhibit
Cat. No. 174114

Half Mummified Head

Half mummified head used for
medical studies in the 1800s.

inside the Vault

RIPLEY'S EXCLUSIVE

FREE FOOT

STYLE BALL

Freestyle football is the artistic sport of performing unbelievable tricks with an American soccer ball.

Performers, called freestylers, creatively juggle a ball with any part of their body, excluding hands and forearms. Freestylers combine dance, acrobatics, and music to entertain and participate in competitions around the world.

John Farnworth

Born and raised in Preston, Lancashire, England,
34-year-old John Farnworth is a multiple freestyle
football world-record holder. Passionate about soccer
from a very young age, he traded the traditional game
with 11 players a side for *futebol de salão*—the five-a-
side variation of the sport popularized in South America.
Farnworth dedicated his time to learning every possible
move and even created his own, developing unique
skills to use as a freestyler. He likes to bend the laws of
physics with just a ball and 100 percent dedication.
In 2018, Farnworth put his skills through a true test of
endurance. He climbed 19,685 ft (6,000 m) up Mount
Everest—all while keeping a ball in the air during the
trek. The 10-day juggling ascent raised money for
the Alzheimer's Society.

Caitlyn Schrepfer

Freestyle football phenom Caitlyn Schrepfer has made the best of a bad situation. Schrepfer began playing soccer at the young age of four, moving into a goalkeeper position as her passion for playing professional soccer grew.

Her dreams of playing professionally came to a halt after an unfortunate hip injury in her teens, but Schrepfer kicked her hobby of freestyle juggling into high gear and shifted her focus to the urban sport. As one of the few females in the male-dominated arena, Caitlyn Schrepfer is the top U.S. female freestyler and is second in the world.

Patrick Shaw

As the youngest competitor in the freestyle football sport, teenager Patrick Shaw is learning to balance high school life with freestyle fame. Taking up the fledgling sport in the eighth grade, Shaw has used his gymnastics and break-dancing background to his advantage. Competing in the Red Bull Street Style 2019, Shaw placed second in the World Finals.

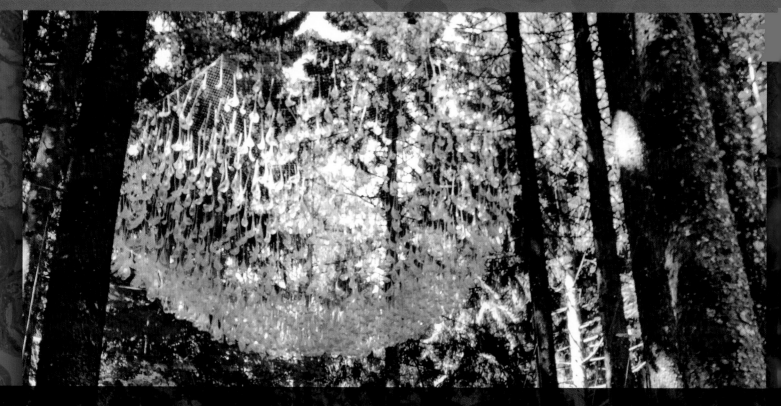

RAIN RESERVOIR

Composed of 5,000 individual clear droplets, this sculpture collects rainwater, which transforms its appearance.

Reservoir, a one-of-a-kind artwork by John Grade, sits in a clearing within an Italian forest. Resembling a delicate chandelier, the sculpture's drops hang suspended by clear nets supported by the trees above. As rainwater or snow gathers within each droplet, the weight of the precipitation creates downward movement, reconfiguring the overall shape of the piece. When dry, the sculpture weighs no more than 70 lb (32 kg), but it can exceed 800 lb (363 kg) when wet.

Up in Arms

The ultimate free-for-all between good and evil (dharma and adharma), the Vijayadashami festival envelopes the Indian countryside in spectacle every autumn. The Vijayadashami is observed in different ways throughout India, but almost all include almsgiving as well as individuals falling into possessed states and fortune-telling. Also in attendance are troupes of people dressed as their favorite deities. Among the most popular is Kali, the goddess of time, creation, destruction, violence, and power, whose many arms symbolize both work and liberation from the Karmic cycles.

BEER BAN
Beer was banned in Iceland from 1915 to March 1, 1989, which has been celebrated there ever since as "Beer Day."

FREE MEAL
When Helen Self ate at the Montana Club Restaurant in Missoula, Montana, on her 109th birthday, she was *paid* $1.25, because the owner offers a percentage discount equal to the celebrant's age.

HISTORIC CAROUSEL
Believed to have been built in 1876, the Flying Horse Carousel at Watch Hill, Rhode Island, still has its original wooden horses with their original agate eyes, although the manes and reins have been replaced. The carousel was declared a National Historic Landmark in 1987. It is now the oldest operating carousel in the United States in which the horses are suspended from chains.

LUNAR POWER
An outside toilet on the shoreline of the Haida Gwaii archipelago off British Columbia, Canada, has a flush that is "powered by the Moon," as the tide washes out the waste twice a day.

FIRST NAMES
Icelandic phone directories list Icelanders alphabetically by their first name rather than their last name.

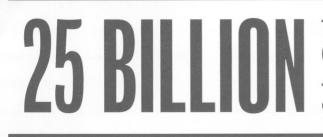

25 BILLION
The number of pairs of waribashi (disposable chopsticks) that are used in Japan each year—equivalent to the amount of timber needed to build 17,000 homes.

TALL TOMATO
A tomato plant grown by Sam Krum in the front yard of his home in Bloomsburg, Pennsylvania, reached a height of 22 ft (6.7 m)—as tall as his house.

RESTAURANT CAPITAL
There are more than 160,000 restaurants in Tokyo, Japan—four times more than in Paris and over five times more than in New York City.

DEVELOPING BEER
SuperEIGHT, a beer created by Dogfish Head Craft Brewery in Delaware, can be used to develop Kodak's Super 8 movie film. Dogfish had the idea after learning that increased levels of acidity and vitamin C in some beers could make them a processing agent for film. The beer contains prickly pear, mango, blackberry, raspberry, boysenberry, elderberry, kiwi, toasted quinoa, and Hawaiian sea salt.

ANGER ROOM
In a special "anger room" in Beijing, China, visitors vent their frustration with life by paying $23 to spend 30 minutes smashing up old household objects with bats and hammers.

TREE AMBULANCE
The Indian city of New Delhi has its own tree ambulance manned by four arboreal experts to treat sick and dying trees.

安心と信頼の創造

READY, SET, PLOW!

Each year, Japan hosts the slowest horse races in the world, where brute strength, rather than speed or agility, takes home the grand prize.

The Tokachi Plain in southeastern Hokkaidō remains a thriving agricultural center dotted with dairy farms and soybean, potato, and wheat fields. Farmers in the area have long relied on the might of Ban'ei (Japanese draft horses) to plow the land. These mighty plow horses first inspired the Ban'ei races in 1946. Today, the races continue with horses pulling heavy sleighs rather than running at a breakneck pace, for a chance at the ¥10 million ($92,260) grand prize.

Ban'ei jockeys often let their horses rest during the race, as the entire sled needs to cross the finish line, and it can weigh up to 1 ton!

SLED RIDE

Since it is built into a cliff, no vehicles are able to access Clovelly in Devon, England, so goods are transported on sleds from the top of the village down the steep cobbled streets to the cottages below.

LOST BOATS

In 2018, New South Wales government marine archaeologist Brad Duncan discovered the wrecks of more than 100 sugar cane boats submerged beneath the surface of Australia's Clarence River.

If you don't pay a hotel bill in Ontario, Canada, the hotel is still permitted by law to sell your horse.

LONG JOURNEY

The only passenger train service out of Darwin in Australia's Northern Territory is the Ghan, which takes three days to complete the 1,851-mi (2,962-km) journey to Adelaide.

SAFE OPTION

The town of Chicken, Alaska, was originally named Ptarmigan after a bird common to the area, but nobody was sure how to spell it, so they agreed on Chicken to avoid embarrassment.

WEDDED ROCKS

Located off the coast of Futami, Japan, a pair of "wedded rocks," or Meoto Iwa, hold a special place in Shinto tradition, symbolizing the holy union that created the spirits of the world.

Besides their joint title, each rock bears a ceremonial name. The larger of the two stands nearly 30 ft (9.1 m) tall and is known as Izanagi, and the smaller measures about 10 ft (3 m) and is named Izanami. A thick rice straw rope with a sacred Shinto braid, or *shimenawa*, encircles them both, binding them together. It's said to weigh at least one ton and gets ceremonially replaced three times a year (due to wave erosion).

Robert Ripley published his drawing of the wedded rocks in the Believe It or Not! cartoon on Sunday, August 3, 1941.

TULIP VODKA

Dutch entrepreneur Joris Putman makes vodka from tulip bulbs and water. It took him two years to perfect the distilling process, using as many as 4,800 bulbs every day, and a bottle of his purest tulip vodka costs around $330.

PAINTED HILLS

Located in the remote outback, the Painted Hills of South Australia are only accessible by airplane and so throughout history they have been seen by no more than a few hundred people. The hills cover an area of 77 sq mi (200 sq km) and boast stunning colors of red, yellow, brown, and white, due to mineral deposits.

GOLDEN BURGER

Patrick Shimada, chef at the Oak Door steakhouse in Tokyo, Japan, created a $900 burger. The Golden Giant Burger features a 2.2-lb (1-kg) patty, Wagyu beef slices, foie gras, shaved truffle, lettuce, cheese, tomatoes, and onions. The bun is 6 in (15 cm) wide and dusted with gold. The whole burger weighs in at 6.6 lbs (3 kg)!

VAST LAKE

With 5,670 cubic mi (23,633 cubic km) of freshwater, Lake Baikal in Russia contains more water than all five of the North American Great Lakes combined. It contains around 20 percent of the world's fresh surface water.

PRISON COURSE

The Louisiana State Penitentiary in Angola has its own nine-hole golf course. The course, which is open to the public, was designed by the prison dentist, Dr. John Ory, and built with prison labor.

GRAVEYARD GIFT

Malaysian Chinese people sometimes visit graveyards at night, bearing gifts in the hope that their dead relatives will yield lucky lottery numbers.

LAST COUNTRY

Women were not allowed to drive in Saudi Arabia until 2018, when the Middle East kingdom became the last country in the world to permit women to get behind the wheel.

FANFEED

DUCK DUCK POTATO

When Dawn Saavedra asked her grandson to pull up some sweet potatoes, she couldn't believe the perfect duck-shaped root that emerged. As Dawn tells Ripley's, the orange tuber in question has everything from a beak, head, and neck to a pair of bumps for wings. It even features a perfectly upturned tail like a mallard. At this point, all the root vegetable in question needs is a set of feathers and a pair of webbed feet.

UNNECESSARY

While it's said that "necessity" is the mother of invention, for artist Matt Benedetto of Burlington, Vermont, all bets are off.

Benedetto uses methods such as 3D printing, sewing, mold making, and more to create what he calls Unnecessary Inventions—fake gadgets that "solve problems that don't really exist by creating products that no one is really asking for." For starters, there's the Cuisine Curtain to conceal open-mouthed chewing. Or how about the Digits Comb for that "I just ran my fingers through my hair" look? There's also a finger extender for extra reach when it comes to your smartphone (or nose). And don't forget the Infinity Saucelet, which lets you keep all of your favorite dipping sauces in one Thanos-inspired location. Finally, Avocado On A Stick looks like deodorant but delivers the perfect slice of avocado toast every time.

DIGITS COMB

CUISINE CURTAIN

INVENTIONS

INFINITY SAUCELET

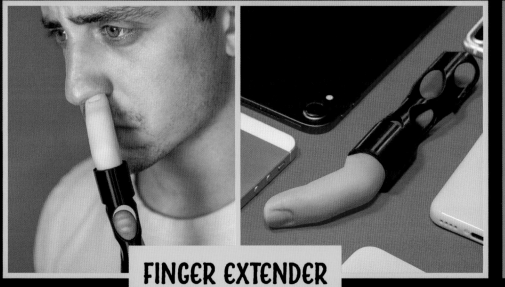

FINGER EXTENDER

AVOCADO STICK

HOME ON THE
STRANGE

Turn off the oven and put down your cookie cutters because someone created what may be the world's tiniest gingerbread house, which is smaller than a human hair!

Travis Casagrande, a research associate at the Canadian Centre for Electron Microscopy, used a focused ion beam microscope to cut the festive house into silicon, going so far as to include a brick chimney, a wreath above the front door, windows, and even a Canadian flag welcome mat. The mini house measures just 10 micrometers long and sits atop what seems to be a giant (but really, it's not) snowman made of research materials like aluminum, cobalt, and nickel.

The tiny snowman with its gingerbread house sitting next to a human hair.

DANCING COCKATOO

Snowball, a sulfur-crested cockatoo, went viral back in 2007 when a video of him dancing to the Backstreet Boys hit the internet. Studies have since shown that Snowball has a repertoire of 14 different dance moves, including head banging and body rolls. Snowball synchronizes his dance moves to the music and shows that he is capable of, among other things, learning, imitation, and mimicking language—something only humans were thought to do.

BASEBALL ANTHEM

The unofficial anthem of American baseball, "Take Me Out to the Ball Game," was written in 1908 by Jack Norworth and Albert Von Tilzer, neither of whom had ever been to a baseball game.

FREE HAIRCUTS

Le Tuan Duong, a barber in Hanoi, Vietnam, offered customers free haircuts in February 2019 if they agreed to cut it in the style of U.S. president Donald Trump or North Korean dictator Kim Jong Un.

PRISON TEAM

The Wyoming State Penitentiary Death Row All Stars was a 1911 baseball team made up of prisoners who were promised reduced sentences, including delays of execution, if they won.

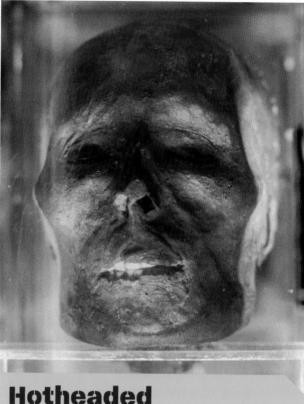

Hotheaded

The remarkably preserved decapitated head of 17th-century martyr St. Oliver Plunkett is displayed in an ornate case inside St. Peter's Church in Drogheda, Ireland. The Roman Catholic Archbishop of Armagh, Plunkett was brutally hanged and then drawn and quartered in London in 1681. His head was thrown into a prepared fire but was quickly retrieved by his friends. The scorch marks from the fire can still be seen on the left side of his face. His head has been housed in the church since 1921, but other parts of his body can be found in England and Germany.

EAR PELLET

Jade Harris was unable to hear out of her left ear for 11 years—until doctors in Devon, England, discovered that she had a BB-gun pellet lodged in it the whole time.

VERY HAIRY

Adult humans have roughly the same number of hairs on their bodies as chimpanzees.

BOOK OPTIONS

If there are 10 books on a bookshelf, they can be arranged in 3,628,800 different ways.

WATER ALLERGY

Maxine Jones, from South Yorkshire, England, has aquagenic urticaria, a rare allergy that causes her to break out in painful blisters if rain or any other moisture touches her skin. As a result, she cannot go out in the rain, she has to wear gloves when brushing her teeth, and she can only take a traditional shower twice a year.

NO EXPERIENCE

Yoshitaka Sakurada, who was appointed Japan's new cybersecurity minister in 2018, had never previously used a computer.

LOST IN TRANSLATION

A supermarket sign in Cwmbran, Wales, that should have read "alcohol-free" in Welsh was replaced after it had been incorrectly translated and was instead offering shoppers "free alcohol."

Bug Blizzard

In August 2019, photojournalist José Antonio Martinez captured surreal images of a blizzard in Navarre, Spain—only instead of floating snowflakes, a frenzy of silken wings fluttered about him. The fuzzy, white orbs were pale burrower mayflies in a frantic rush to mate and lay eggs in the River Ebro before dying.

RADISH FESTIVAL

Held annually on December 23 in Oaxaca, Mexico, Noche de Los Rábanos, or Night of the Radishes, is a Christmastime festival dedicated to the artistic carving of radishes!

Radishes are a classic component of Oaxaca's Christmas cuisine, both as an ingredient and a decorative garnish. The radish carving contest dates back to 1897 and was used as a fun way of promoting local agriculture. Participants use knives and toothpicks to carve the vegetables into imaginative sculptures of buildings, figures, and scenes.

SAND JAM

Two years, 330 tons of sand, and $1 million later, artist Leandro Erlich unveiled a massive art installation in Miami Beach, Florida, comprised of 66 life-sized cars in a traffic jam.

Erlich described the artwork as a future relic and a commentary on the dangers that Florida's fragile ecosystems face due to rising sea levels and climate change.

18,818

The number of cupcakes assembled in a cupcake tower standing 41.7 ft (12.7 m) tall in a shopping mall in Chennai, India.

SUBGLACIAL LAKE

Buried under a sheet of ice 3,500 ft (1,067 m) thick in the Antarctic, the subglacial Lake Mercer is more than twice the size of Manhattan. It covers an area of 62 sq mi (160 sq km) and is one of 400 lakes beneath the Antarctic ice.

OYSTER PEARL

Rick Antosh, from Edgewater, New Jersey, found a rare $4,000 pearl while eating an oyster at Grand Central Oyster Bar in New York City on December 5, 2018. The restaurant sells more than 5,000 oysters on the half shell every day, but this was only the second time a pearl has been found there in 28 years.

GPS NIGHTMARE

The municipality of Hilgermissen in northwest Germany has 2,200 residents but no street names. There have been no street names for more than 40 years, and in a 2019 referendum, residents voted to keep it like that, instead advising visitors to navigate their way around by using local landmarks.

NARROW STREET

Vinárna Čertovka, a pedestrian-only street in Prague, Czech Republic, is so narrow that traffic lights have been installed at either end to stop people from bumping into each other. The 33-ft-long (10-m) street, which runs between houses near the famous Charles Bridge, is only 20 in (50 cm) wide, making it impossible for two people to pass. So the lights signal whether the street is empty of people or occupied. When a large German tourist became stuck there, her body had to be smeared with soap so that so she could slide free.

SAUNA CAR

Willem Maesalu, of Tallinn, Estonia, has converted his Audi 100 Avant car into a sauna. He has fitted it with traditional sauna features, including wooden interior panels, thermometers, and a wood-fired stove next to the steering wheel. To use the sauna, he inserts a chimney into the car's hood, fires up the wood stove, and heats it to a maximum of 140°F (60°C), because if it got any hotter the car's windows would crack.

FOOD WASTE

Due to a shortage of space in landfills, the Chinese city of Jinan disposes of food waste by feeding it to a billion cockroaches. Housed in a special building, the roaches are fed around 50 tons of kitchen waste every day—that's equivalent to the weight of seven adult elephants.

PURL JAM

Combining two of Finland's favorite pastimes, the first Heavy Metal World Knitting Championships were held in Joensuu in July 2019. Competitors knitted to the beat of loud rock music, with needles moving rhythmically like air guitars. According to organizers, there are 50 heavy metal bands per 100,000 people in Finland, where hundreds of thousands of people also enjoy knitting and needlecraft.

TOP ATTRACTION

The top-rated attraction in Bude, Cornwall, England, on the website Tripadvisor is a 230-ft-long (70-m) covered plastic tunnel that connects a supermarket to its car park to protect shoppers from rain.

Ripley's Exhibit
Cat. No. 169974

Lily Slippers

In ancient China, daughters of
wealthy families purposely broke
and bound their feet. The ideal
foot was 4 in (10.16 cm) long
and was crushed into a shape
resembling a lotus flower. These
slippers are cream, mint green,
and lavender, with a black trim
on the top and navy heels.

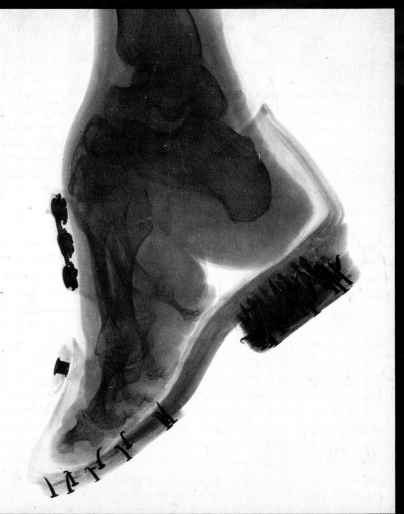

Here is an X-ray of a Chinese woman's foot,
showing the effects of foot binding. This
scan was taken in the 1920s, and today only
a handful of women still have bound feet.

Ripley's Exhibit

Cat. No. 11532

Conch Shell Trumpet

This Tibetan conch shell trumpet was used by priests to summon the devoted to service. The conch used to make this trumpet is a testimony to the ancient trade routes of the Far East. Tibet lies hundreds of miles from the nearest ocean, yet a sea shell native to the South Pacific Ocean wound up in a temple monastery in Lhasa, Tibet.

inside the vault

FRONT VIEW

BACK VIEW

Selling the Time

Ruth Belville made a living selling time to the people of London! Ruth inherited the business from her father, John, who launched the service in 1836. Each morning, he visited the Greenwich Observatory and set his watch before heading out by buggy to adjust the clocks of more than 200 clients. Upon his death in 1856, his widow Maria took up the business, and Ruth continued from 1892 until the beginning of World War II, when bombings made the streets too dangerous to traverse.

COMMITMENT ISSUES

Colorado once had three governors in 24 hours. On March 16, 1905, Democrat Alva Adams was forced to resign because of election improprieties and was replaced by his Republican opponent James H. Peabody, who the next day agreed to step aside in favor of his lieutenant governor, Jesse F. McDonald.

CHRISTMAS TREE

Aileen Stirling's family, from Renfrew, Scotland, have decorated the same ornamental Christmas tree for more than 100 years.

GROCERY COUPON

A shopper at a grocery store in Mineola, New York, saved 20 cents on some Crisco oil in 2019 by using a 36-year-old coupon with no expiration date.

SIGNIFICANT NUMBER

The baby daughter of Erin and Mike Potts, of Hugo, Minnesota, was born at 11:11 p.m. on November 11, 2018—the 11th day of the 11th month.

HIGH SCORE

A football game in Iowa between Thomas Jefferson High School and Sioux City North High School on August 31, 2018, ended in a 99-81 win for Thomas Jefferson High— the highest-scoring game in the history of Iowa high school football.

Water on Wheels

French artist Benedetto Bufalino recently transformed an old public transportation bus into a one-of-a-kind swimming pool. Located outside Lens in northern France, the bus-turned-pool required serious retrofitting to make it a safe, durable public swimming facility. After removing the side of the bus and emptying the interior, Bufalino resurfaced it with a smooth, waterproof material and even added seats and a lifeguard station. Voilà! The revamped bus now enjoys a second life as a hub of summer fun.

TWISTED CREATIONS

Japanese artist Masayoshi Matsumoto crafts intricate animals and insects from balloons.

The self-taught artist's creations take between two and six hours to complete. To make the lifelike designs, he weaves and ties the balloons together in innovative ways. Matsumoto refuses to use other materials to construct his balloon creations. This means no markers, adhesives, or embellishments go into crafting each masterpiece.

FLOATING FRENCHMAN

In 2019, Jean-Jacques Savin, a 72-year-old Frenchman, completed a transatlantic crossing in a barrel-shaped orange container.

Setting off from Spain's Canary Islands in late December, he allowed ocean currents alone to propel him. After 122 days floating at sea, he entered the Caribbean on April 27, marking the completion of his journey. All told, he traveled more than 2,800 mi (4500 km), surviving on freeze-dried food, freshly caught fish, foie gras, and two bottles of wine. His handmade craft measured 10 ft (3 m) long and 7 ft (2.1 m) wide, and included a porthole in the floor to watch fish swim and extra reinforcement to counter orca attacks.

WINE NOT?

10,000 varieties of wine grapes exist worldwide.

At more than 1,600 years old and dating back to the 4th century, the Speyer wine bottle (also called the Römerwein) is the world's oldest bottle of wine.

The oak trees used to create wine barrels are likely almost 200 years old.

Former U.S. president
Abraham Lincoln once worked
as a bartender.

There are more than 500
different species of oak trees,
but only three are suitable for
wine barrel production—French,
European, and American.

Red grapes can be used to create white
wine. Since both red and white grapes
produce the same clear-colored juice,
if the red grape skin isn't used during
fermentation, the juice from red grapes
can become white wine.

UNDERWATER SPIDER
Diving bell spiders live underwater and even weave silk webs between aquatic vegetation. They only need to come up for air once a day, when they collect an air bubble at the surface and trap it in the dense layer of hairs on their abdomen and legs. They then dive down again and release the bubble into their web, allowing them to breathe and eat underwater.

NATIVE BATS
Three species of bats—the long-tailed bat and two species of short-tailed bats—are New Zealand's only native land mammals.

CAT TREADMILL
Korean start-up Pet Ding has invented a treadmill wheel for cats so that they can exercise even when their owners are away. The device features an integrated LED lamp, like a laser pen, that moves in time with the wheel, which the cat instinctively follows.

DISTANT DOG
Workers on an oil rig in the Gulf of Thailand spotted a dog swimming in the sea 135 mi (217 km) from shore. After the dog was rescued, he was given the name Boonrod, which means "the saved one."

TOXIC MILLIPEDE
The 1.2-in-long (3-cm), shocking pink dragon millipede from Southeast Asia stores toxic cyanide in its glands and shoots it at would-be predators. The poison is so potent that it can cause death to a small animal within a minute.

NON-WALKERS
Despite having six legs like any other insect, dragonflies are not great walkers. But they can use their legs to perch on flower stems or tree branches and also to form a "basket" to catch bugs in midair.

STRONG SPIDER

Two Australian men stumbled across a gruesome find while doing light repair work in Tasmania: a gigantic huntsman spider devouring a dead pygmy possum.

According to the wife of one of the men, Justine Latton, they were making repairs at an old ski lodge in Mount Field National Park. Suddenly, they noticed a spider the size of a large human hand nibbling on the diminutive mammal. Latton shared her husband's photo of the horrific scene, which quickly went viral on social media and caused some commenters to label it the "stuff of nightmares." Others identified the long-legged spider as a member of the *Sparassidae* family, also known as a giant crab spider.

DINNER'S READY!

SHARK CAUGHT FISH!

BIRD CAUGHT SHARK!

Food Chain

One osprey bit off more than it could chew after snatching a small shark that happened to be in the middle of eating a fish. West Florida photographer Doc Jon couldn't believe his eyes when he zoomed in on images he'd just taken of an osprey with a fish in its talons. Upon closer inspection, he realized the "fish" was actually a 1-ft-long (0.3-m) blacktip or nurse shark with a large fish in its mouth.

RUDE WELCOME
When firefighters in London, England, tried to rescue Jessie, a blue and yellow macaw that had spent three days on the roof of a house, the bird swore at them!

POOP SAND
Parrotfish feed on coral, and after eating the digestible parts, they excrete the indigestible parts as tiny grains of sand. A single humphead parrotfish can produce 200 lb (90 kg) of sand each year, and nearly every grain of sand on Hawaii's white beaches is actually fish poop.

WRESTLING MATCH
Two male pythons were so preoccupied with fighting each other over a female that they fell three stories from the roof of a house in Cooroy, Queensland, Australia. After landing safely, the victorious python slithered back up two floors to take up residence behind a cane couch on the veranda.

LAVISH FUNERAL
After Captain, Sasha Smajic's 11-year-old Staffordshire bull terrier, died on Christmas Day 2018, the dog was given a $5,500 funeral in Hertfordshire, England, complete with horse-drawn hearse, a limo, and a release of doves. He also had his name spelled out in flowers.

GREAT ESCAPE
A group of chimpanzees used a tree branch that had been felled by a storm to make a ladder and escape from their enclosure at Belfast Zoo in Northern Ireland.

ROLE REVERSALS

Despite normally eating vegetation, snowshoe hares of the Canadian Yukon have been found to eat meat from animal carcasses, including that of a lynx—the hare's natural predator.

Frogs usually eat bugs, but a species of ground beetle larvae turns the tables when a hungry amphibian tries to eat it. Instead of getting swallowed, the larvae latches on to its would-be predator and starts eating it!

In 1983, scientists introduced 1,000 lobsters to an area covered in whelks—a type of sea snail lobsters like to eat—but were shocked when the whelks overwhelmed the lobsters and ate them all within 30 minutes!

JUMPING BULL
Sabine Rouas, a horse trainer from Strasbourg, France, rides a 1.3-ton bull named Aston over equestrian fences. The bull can jump obstacles up to 3.28 ft (1 m) high with Rouas on his back and has learned to trot, gallop, and jump like a horse by watching her train his friend, Sammy the pony.

WIDE ARTERIES
A blue whale's arteries are so large that a small child could theoretically swim through them.

GUANO HARVEST
During the American Civil War, bat caves in the South were harvested for their poop in order to make gunpowder. Bat guano consists largely of saltpeter, a major ingredient in explosives.

EYE POKING
Capuchin monkeys create a sense of trust by poking each other in the eye. One monkey will sometimes stick his finger inside the eyelid of another and hold it there for a while to find out whether the second monkey trusts him not to cause any pain.

LEMUR YOGA
At Armathwaite Hall in Cumbria, England, humans practice yoga among lemurs, who often imitate the poses.

CANNIBAL COBRA
Up to 40 percent of the southern African Cape cobra's diet consists of other snakes—and sometimes other Cape cobras.

AQUACULTURE

Deep beneath the surface of France's Thau Basin, more than 750 shellfish producers cultivate oysters on collector lines—like this one that's tended by aquaculturist Jean-Christophe Cabrol.

Despite its high salinity, the Étang du Thau (Thau Basin) is classified as the second largest lake in France. Grand Central for the nation's oyster farming industry, more than 2,750 oyster tables produce 14,330 tons of shellfish here annually. These oysters account for 8.5 percent of France's total oyster consumption, and due to the excellent water quality, they can be eaten within minutes of harvesting.

FAN FEED

CRAFTY CATCHER

Barry Osborn of Granbury, Texas, sent Ripley's these photos, telling us, "I spent more than 50 hours building a functioning rod and reel using nothing but over 1,500 pipe cleaners." Believe it or not, Osborn is the recipient of more than 300 fishing awards and records. According to the Texas Parks and Wildlife Department, he holds more state records than any other person in history—a whopping 78 to be exact. He hopes to catch a record-breaking fish with the pipe cleaner rod and reel next!

UNIQUE CONDITION

Hamish Robinson, a 10-year-old from Manchester, England, is the only person in the world known to have a specific genetic disorder. The unique defect, which has caused him to have a functioning kidney at the top of his right thigh, has been named "Hamish syndrome" after him.

MICROSCOPIC AD

Dutch manufacturing company ASML created a micro advertisement that was smaller than the width of a human hair. This made it three times smaller than the ad produced by U.S. fast-food chain Arby's, who printed one on a sesame seed from a burger bun.

LIGHTNING STRIKE

Josiah Wiedman, age 13, was thrown 9 ft (2.7 m) into the air after being struck by a bolt of lightning in El Mirage, Arizona. His heart stopped beating for a whole minute, but he survived because the skateboard he was carrying channeled most of the voltage into the ground instead of his body.

TWO for ONE

Angler Steve Glum, of Ocoee, Florida, landed two bass on one hook in February 2019. Both fish were released safely.

MULTIPLE FLIGHTS

So that he could spend Christmas 2018 with his daughter Pierce, who was working as a flight attendant for Delta Air Lines, Hal Vaughan, from Ocean Springs, Mississippi, bought tickets to fly with her as a passenger on all six of her flights on Christmas Eve and Christmas Day.

MONSTER FATBERG

A 210-ft-long (64-m) fatberg discovered in the sewers of Sidmouth, Devon, England, in 2019 was bigger than the Leaning Tower of Pisa. The congealed mass of waste came from local drains and toilets and had to be broken up using pickaxes and high-pressure water jets.

TIED RESULT

The winner of the 2018 mayor's race in Peachland, British Columbia, Canada, was decided by a lucky draw after two candidates tied with 804 votes each. Cindy Fortin's name was pulled out of the box first, and so she defeated Harry Gough and was elected to serve a four-year term.

LOOK ALIVE!

Despite dying more than 2,000 years ago, the mummy of Lady Xin Zhui remains one of the best preserved in the world, complete with type-A blood in her veins and skin soft to the touch.

She died in 163 BC, but Xin Zhui's body could have been brought to the morgue yesterday. Her skin feels moist and elastic, her ligaments flexible, and she boasts her original hair, eyebrows, and eyelashes. Discovered in 1971, her burial contained more than 1,000 artifacts, including 162 carved wooden figures of servants. But what shocked archaeologists most was Xin Zhui's physical condition, the result of an elaborate, airtight tomb.

A recreation of what Xin Zhui may have looked like when she was alive more than 2,000 years ago.

Marital Duels

In his 15th-century account of trials by combat, Hans Talhoffer describes brutal marital duels of medieval Europe. Unlike today's splitting spouses who arm themselves with lawyers, unhappy Germanic couples once brandished clubs and rocks. Talhoffer's detailed descriptions and illustrations of battle strategies clearly indicate that such fights happened with enough frequency to warrant a tactical manual.

The husbands were buried in a pit to make the fight more fair!

EWWW!

Spidey Snack

A native of Puerto Ayacucho in the Venezuelan Amazon, chef Nelson Mendez has spent the past 20 years pairing European culinary traditions with ingredients from the Amazonian pantry. The result? A one-of-a-kind Venezuelan gastronomic experience not for the faint of heart. Since 90 percent of all creatures living in the rainforest are arthropods, Mendez's "creepy crawly haute cuisine" boasts recipes for cooked spiders, insects, and much more.

BIG BEAR

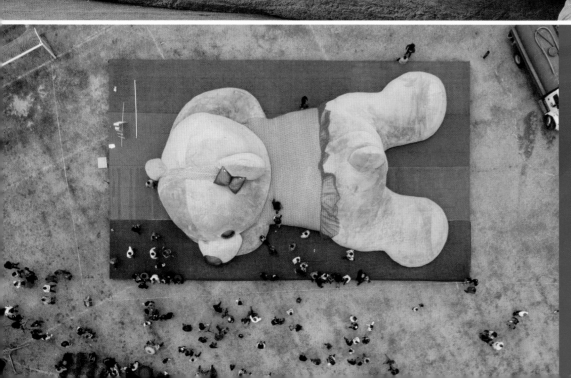

Residents of Xonacatlán, Mexico, spent more than three months stitching together a nearly 65-ft-long (20-m) teddy bear.

The enormous stuffed bear, named Xonita, weighed 4.4 tons—more than the weight of a full-grown male hippo. Xonacatlán is considered the stuffed animal capital of Mexico, as there are literally dozens of plush toy manufacturers in the small city.

Witchy Waters

"Keep Portland Weird" has become the iconic mantra for Oregon's most populous city, located along the banks of the Willamette River. But even local Portlanders were caught craning their necks when hundreds of witches traded in their broomsticks for paddleboards, traveling 6 mi (10 km) down the Willamette River. The pointy-hatted aquatic parade paddled to promote a local nonprofit clothes drive, making Portland that much weirder in the process.

KIMONO COLLECTION

Takako Yoshino, from Nagoya, Japan, has a collection of more than 4,500 kimono sashes, known as Obi.

EARLY START

Switzerland's Mathilde Gremaud, who won the gold in the Women's Ski Big Air category at the 2019 Winter X Games in Aspen, Colorado, started skiing when she was only two years old.

HUMAN PYRAMID

The Rock Aqua Jays, a waterskiing team from Janesville, Wisconsin, formed and maintained an 80-person human pyramid on water for a distance of 1,148 ft (350 m).

Charlie O'Brien, 16, spent 33 hours straight on a playground swing in Hawke's Bay, New Zealand.

FEET FEAT

Using both hands as well as his feet, 13-year-old Que Jianyu, from Xiamen, China, solved three Rubik's Cubes at the same time, completing the challenge in 1 minute 36.4 seconds. He has also solved a single Rubik's Cube in 15.8 seconds while hanging upside down.

FRIENDLY PIGGYBACK

For more than six years, 12-year-old Xu Bingyang has been carrying his classmate, Zhang Ze, around Hebazi Town Central Primary School in Meishan, China. Zhang has a medical condition that makes it difficult for him to walk unaided, so Xu carries him to the toilet, to lunch, or to his next class.

What the Deck?

Sean Oulashin of Portland, Oregon, can shuffle a deck of cards like no one else! He practices the art of cardistry, which he describes as an "aesthetically pleasing" method of shuffling cards. He can cut the deck into several stacks, flipping and spinning them in a mesmerizing dance. One of his most impressive tricks is when he slings a card from the deck, only for it to fly around him in a circle and land back in his hands! See for yourself on his Instagram account: @notseano

IN THEIR OWN WORDS

Artist Phil Vance of Sonora, California, creates masterpieces entirely from handwritten text.

His elaborate portraits honor historical figures like Mark Twain, Einstein, and Picasso. But his methods are anything but ordinary. Vance relies on the written word, like cross-hatching, for color, texture, and patterns. Taken from inspiring quotes, the words get repeated thousands of times in different sizes and layers. They create shadows, contours, and details. Like pointillist paintings, the words blend into one image from a distance. But up close, they fragment into phrases, as if the viewer is peering into the thoughts of each subject.

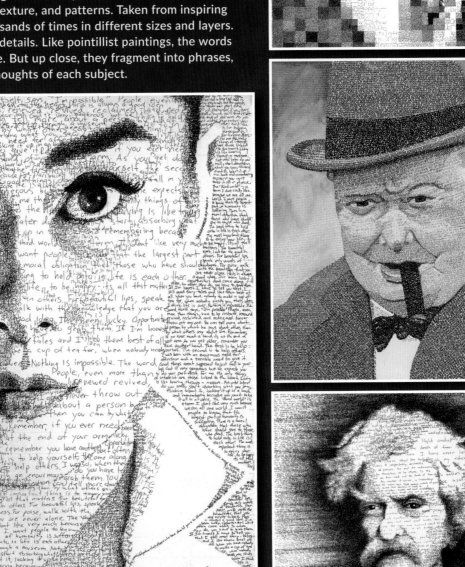

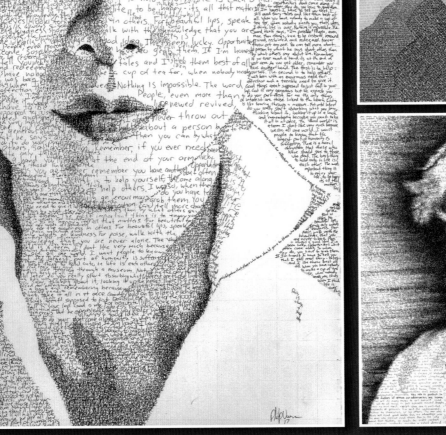

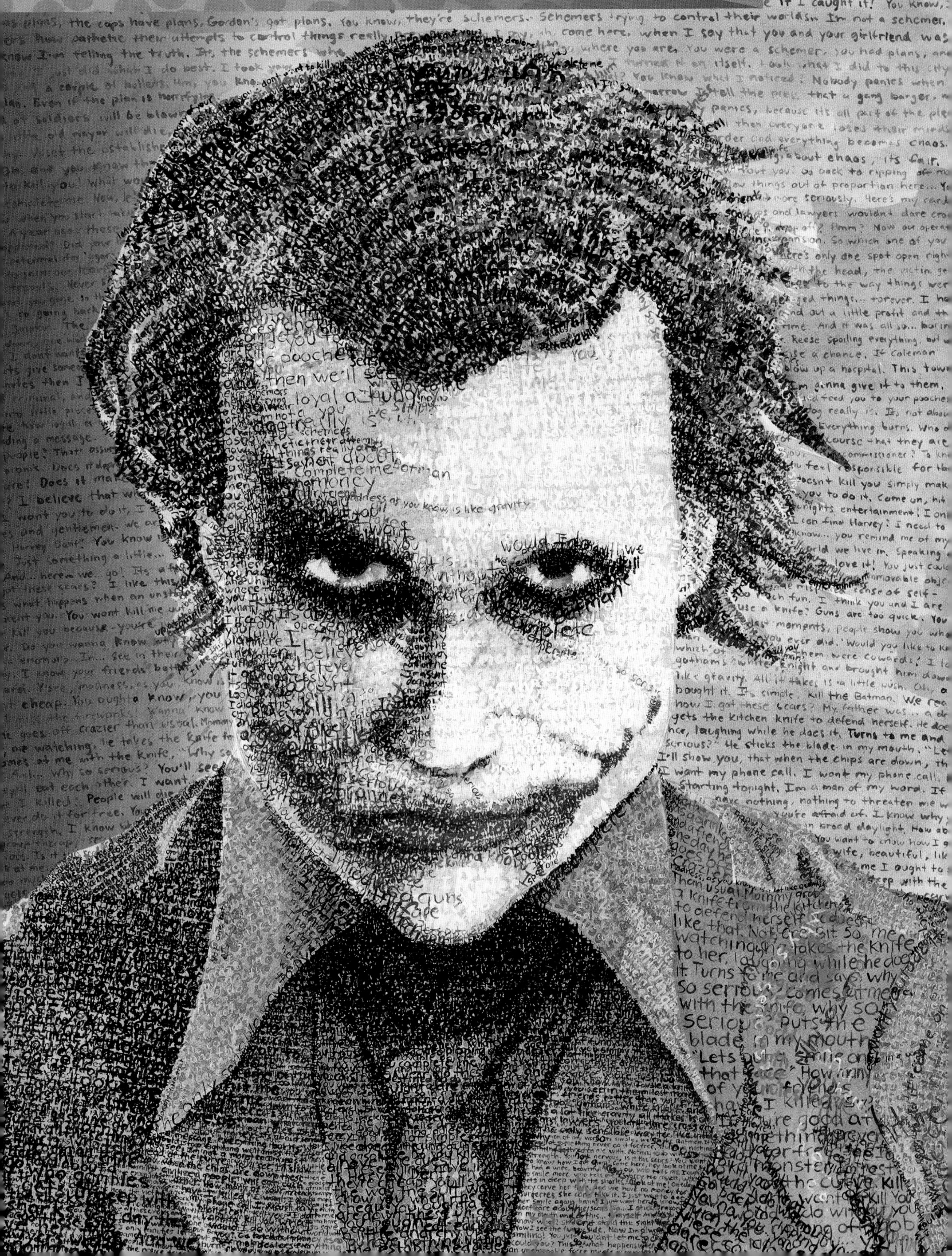

HAZARDOUS HARVEST

The Norse tradition of collecting seabird eggs along Iceland's rugged coastline still leads to cliffhangers.

Iceland is known for stunning birdlife, from Arctic terns to Atlantic puffins. These birds take advantage of the nation's rugged coastal cliffs for natural protection while nesting. People have been harvesting eggs from these cliffs for hundreds of years! And while it is no longer necessary for survival, some hardy locals, like Jón Arnar Beck, still engage in the practice. Today, it involves safety harnesses, radio equipment, and a four-by-four truck. But the dizzying heights remain intimidating. To protect the bird population, local authorities make sure harvesters leave plenty of eggs in the nests so they can hatch.

COLLECTORS
SHINE A LIGHT
THROUGH THE EGGS TO
MAKE SURE THEY ARE
FRESHLY LAID.

Ripley's Exhibit
Cat. No. 169383

Dodo Bird Skeleton Cast

There are only a few historical paintings and drawings of the extinct dodo bird and even fewer taxidermy specimens. The cast shown here was made from the most complete specimen ever found (in a cave on Mauritius in 2007).

From its fat, round body to its distinctively bulbous, hooked beak, the flightless dodo bird was found only on the island of Mauritius in the Indian Ocean and was first recorded by Dutch sailors in 1598. It had no means of protection from man or the dogs that sailors brought with them, and living on an isolated island, it knew no fear. Though its flesh wasn't particularly tasty, its eggs were. Less than 100 years after the dodo bird's discovery, it was extinct.

Carved Egg
Jewelry Box

Jewelry box made from a white rhea eggshell. A rhea is a large flightless bird of South America. Created and hand-decorated by Pat Beason.

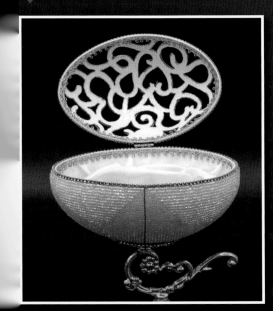

Scrimshaw Ostrich Egg

Whalers would once engrave nautical scenes upon bone or ivory in a practice called "scrimshaw." This beautiful scene was carved into the shell of an ostrich egg, which, despite it being an egg shell, is a **very** sturdy material.

Top view

JUMPING LIKE A HORSE

Sixteen-year-old Ava Vogel of Canada runs and jumps like a horse to stay in shape!

Not only does Ava gallop and trot around on all fours, but she jumps hurdles and obstacles, too. The self-described horse lover says the activity brings her closer to her four-legged friends. Believe it or not, she hasn't sustained any serious injuries from the hobby—just a few minor strains and sprains. Her skills have earned her more than 50,000 followers on Instagram! Ripley's caught up with Ava so she could tell us more about this unique sport.

Q: WHAT'S THE COMMUNITY LIKE?
A: I started this about eight years ago when I saw other people online doing this. I made my Instagram account and was instantly welcomed into the community, though I was not that good. I quickly made lots of friends and learned the horselike movements. The small community is still as welcoming as ever! I know many other jumpers online and in real life.

Q: WHAT ARE YOUR GOALS?
A: In jumping, my main goal is to inspire others! It's a great feeling to see that I've inspired others the way I was inspired back in 2012. But I also hope to reach new jumping records. In school, I hope to study kinesiology.

Q: WHAT IS YOUR FAVORITE JUMP AND GAIT?
A: My favorite jump has to be the Liverpool aka "open water" fence. It's so much fun to gallop up to it and spring myself in the air. My favorite gait is the canter because I can do the most things with it—like lead changes, pirouettes, and jumps. I also find it the easiest.

Q: WHAT TYPE OF TERRAIN DO YOU PREFER?
A: I prefer to run and jump on grass. It's the softest, and the ground is a little more cushioned than carpet or tile.

Q: WHAT IS THE OFFICIAL NAME OF "JUMPING LIKE A HORSE"?
A: Most people, including me, call it "Jumping Like a Horse," but others call it quadrobics or human horse jumping.

FAKE PHONES
Armed street robberies are so common in Mexico City that people there have started buying specially designed fake $20 smartphones to hand over to muggers.

COMPUTER ERROR
Due to a computer error, New York resident Tommy Straub was sent a $38 million utility bill for his small New York studio apartment. His bill normally runs around $74.

BUG EATER
Marcela Iglesias, from Los Angeles, California, eats five live Chinese weevils every day to keep healthy. She either swallows them raw or takes them with a glass of water. The bugs are a good source of protein, and she hopes they may also help combat digestive problems and chronic pain.

Wallace's giant bee—an insect the size of a human thumb—was rediscovered on an island in Indonesia in 2019—38 years after it was believed to have become extinct.

BUG ATTACK
The Rogers County Courthouse in Oklahoma was evacuated in February 2019 when a lawyer arrived with dozens of bedbugs falling off his suit. The courtroom was soon overrun with the blood-sucking insects, forcing all business to be cancelled for the day.

ROACH INSULT
For Valentine's Day in 2019, the Hemsley Conservation Centre in Sevenoaks, England, offered spurned lovers the chance to pay $2 to name cockroaches after their former partners.

PRIZED POOP
Jars of poop from 1997 Kentucky Derby winning racehorse Silver Charm went on sale in 2019 for $200 each.

Cello, Honey!

More than 20,000 honey bees have taken up residence in a reclaimed cello as part of the aptly titled music project Bee Hive Cello. The musical project is headed up by Dr. Martin Bencsik, a professor for Nottingham Trent University. Bencsik got the idea for the project from his wife, a professional cellist, and hopes to study sounds and vibrations made by the bees via the reclaimed instrument. Bencsik has collaborated on an album using recordings of the bees in the cello to raise awareness about the plight of bees and other pollinating insects.

DO YOU WANT FRIES WITH THAT?

FOOD DOs

Off The Grid

Residents and visitors to the Bellevue neighborhood in Saint-Herblain, France, got a serious eyeful when an actor from the French street theater company Royal de Luxe decided to set up camp nearly 33 ft (10 m) off the ground on the side of a building. Performing the role of the eccentric Monsieur Bourgogne, the actor sat in the entrance of his tent surrounded by a picnic table, bags of potato chips, and a whimsical assortment of other camping-related props.

An Australian hairdresser has raised tens of thousands of dollars for the Make-A-Wish Foundation by transforming people's hair into items from a fast-food menu.

Most people get picky when it comes to finding a hair in their food, but what if your hair *is* food? That's the predicament that customers of hairdresser Mykey O'Halloran find themselves in. But it's all for a good cause. O'Halloran transforms volunteers' hair into everything from hamburgers to cheesy fries to raise money for charity.

A HAIL OF A
STORM

MEXICO IN SUMMER!

On June 30, 2019, the 1.5 million residents of Guadalajara, Mexico, awoke to layers of icy hail several feet thick that had blanketed the city's streets, damaging cars and buildings.

It's not unusual for Guadalajara to see summer temperatures of 90°F (32°C) or more, but in this strange instance, ten people were treated for hypothermia because of the freakiest weather phenomenon in recent memory. The Mexican Army and local authorities deployed heavy machinery to dig residents out of the slushy mess. The curiosity turned into chaos as the hailstones melted into floodwaters powerful enough to sweep cars away.

FAN FEED

Star-Spangled Lawn

J. R. Majewski of Port Clinton, Ohio, showed us how he honored veterans in his area by painting a 5,000 sq ft (465 sq m) American flag on his lawn. It took him 12 hours to complete, and he used biodegradable chalk, making it eco-friendly art. As for the Betsy Ross–inspired version of the flag with 13 stars? Majewski says he chose it for practical reasons, "Painting 50 perfect stars would have been much more time-consuming and expensive."

MAGIC FORMULA
Romanian economist and math expert Stefan Mandel used his own formula to win the lottery 14 times.

LUXURY DONUT
Enter Through the Donut Shop, a restaurant in Miami Beach, Florida, celebrated its grand opening with a $100 donut containing 24-karat gold and Cristal champagne.

HIDDEN MOUNTAIN
Brazil's highest mountain, the 9,827-ft-high (2,996-m) Pico da Neblina, was not discovered until the 1950s because it is almost permanently shrouded in dense clouds. Located on the edge of the Amazon basin near the border with Venezuela, the mountain is said to have first been spotted by an airplane pilot who happened to fly over it in a rare clear moment when it was not hidden from view.

LAZINESS MUSEUM
In 2008, a Museum of Laziness opened for a week in Bogotá, Colombia. Visitors were invited to laze around in hammocks, in beds, or in front of the TV, anything so that they could avoid work.

WELL READ
India produces more than 17,000 daily newspapers in 188 registered languages plus 39,000 journals and weeklies.

$560
The amount Pinheads Pizza in Dublin, Ireland, pays to any customer who can finish its 32-in (81-cm) pizza and two milkshakes in under 32 minutes.

MALL FLEET
Between 1985 and 2005, a water ride attraction at West Edmonton Shopping Mall had as many submarines as the entire Canadian Navy.

UNDERWATER CARVING
Scuba divers working 30 ft (9 m) below the surface in the Florida Keys take part in an annual underwater pumpkin carving contest for Halloween.

PIPE BANDS
There are more Scottish pipe bands per capita in New Zealand than in Scotland itself.

WITCHES BEWARE
"Witch windows" on houses in Vermont are positioned at an angle of 45 degrees because it was believed that witches could not fly their broomsticks through tilted windows.

ALCOHOLIC SORBET
Buzz Pop Cocktails—a range of Italian sorbets—contain an alcohol content comparable to beer, meaning a person can actually get drunk on ice pops.

PSYCHOLOGICAL TEST
Anyone who fails their driving test four times in Switzerland must undergo a psychological assessment before being allowed to try again.

HOPPIN' BOTTLES

LadyBEAST, a circus artist based out of New Orleans, Louisiana, stuns audiences with her aerial bottle-walking feats.

Balanced atop thin-necked champagne bottles, LadyBEAST walks and dances with ease. Yet she leaves audiences breathless, and the feats of illusion and magic don't stop there. She also specializes in Houdini-style performances, where her escape artistry puts crowds on the edges of their seats. Her hoop-dangling feats are also renowned in the circus arts world.

15.5 in
(39 cm)

In 2018, LadyBEAST became the first woman to escape a straitjacket hanging by her ankles from a hot-air balloon. The hot-air balloon hoisted her nearly 100 ft (30 m) into the air—10 stories high—and after escaping, she hung by her elbow and descended safely to the ground without any of her safety harnesses.

100 ft
(30 m)

LadyBEAST's chair stack stand sees her climb atop three wooden chairs and then balance precariously atop her tallest bottle. Ripley's measured her height to be 12 ft 3 in (3.7 m) above the ground! Her height record is now even taller.

During LadyBEAST's TEDx talk, she explained, "I take very calculated risks. I rely on my muscle memory, on my training, and the understanding of my craft in order to catch myself from my fall."

12 ft 3 in
(3.7 m)

TERRITORIAL TEARS
The small African antelope called the dik-dik marks its territory with tears. It ducks its head into long grass and uses the stems to spread a sticky secretion from the corners of its eyes in order to make other animals aware of its presence.

PET SNAIL
Magdalena Dusza, from Krakow, Poland, has a giant African snail named Misiek as a pet. This species of snail can reach 8 in (20 cm) or more in length, but Magdalena loves cuddling with it on the sofa and doesn't even mind when it covers her body in slime.

MONKEY MEAL
A 10-ft-long (3-m) Komodo dragon, native to Indonesia, was filmed eating a live monkey whole in just six gulps. The giant lizards have been known to devour prey almost 80 percent their own body size. They have a venomous bite delivered with shark-like teeth and have occasionally been responsible for human deaths.

SUPER HEARING
Elephants can hear thunderstorms from up to 150 mi (241 km) away and can hear even better by lifting one leg off the ground. In addition to using their huge ears, they listen with their feet, which are highly sensitive and can detect distant communications from other elephants through the ground. Raising one foot to face the source of the sound helps them listen more attentively.

DISTANT HOME
For over half a century, up to 100 wallabies have lived naturally on Lambay Island off the east coast of Ireland—despite being almost 10,000 mi (16,000 km) from their native land of Australia.

SINGING SEAL
Scientists at the University of St. Andrews in Scotland taught a gray seal named Zola to sing "Twinkle, Twinkle, Little Star" and the theme to Star Wars.

SURPRISE PASSENGER
A spotted python traveled more than 9,000 mi (14,484 km) from Queensland, Australia, to Glasgow, Scotland, inside airline passenger Moira Boxall's shoe. The shoe was in her suitcase when she returned home to Scotland from a vacation in Australia.

HUNGRY GOATS
Ventura County Fire Department in California hired hundreds of hungry goats in 2019 to eat dried brush that presented a fire hazard.

Wasp vs. Spider

This huntsman spider isn't going to be just a tasty treat—an adversarial tarantula hawk wasp has far more sinister plans. The hawk wasp's venom works as a paralytic, immobilizing the spider while it is dragged to the wasp's nest. Once there, the wasp will lay parasitic eggs in the body of the incapacitated spider. And after the larvae hatch, they will devour their way out of the spider over the course of several weeks.

Ghostly Gators

Gatorland, an outdoor theme park and wildlife preserve in Orlando, Florida, recently revealed some new residents—three adorable albino alligator babies. Each one displays beautiful pink and white markings. The color is rare in the wild because it causes the reptiles to stand out, making it hard for them to survive.

UN CORN PUPPY

Narwhal the puppy has an extra tail growing out of the middle of his forehead and is helping to raise awareness about rescue animals.

Employees at Mac's Mission, an animal rescue center in Missouri for special needs animals, named the darling doggy after a species of whale that has a single tusk growing from its forehead like a unicorn. A thorough veterinarian examination has determined there is "no medical need to remove" the extra tail—a feature that many online fans agree makes Narwhal the "coolest puppy ever."

HAGGIS HURLING

Contestants at the Bearsden Milngavie Highland Games in Scotland compete to see who can throw haggis the farthest, sometimes tossing it more than 200 ft (61 m)!

Haggis, Scotland's national dish, is made with sheep organs. If you'd rather chuck this dish than taste it, haggis hurling may just be your sport. Contestants take turns climbing atop an overturned whiskey barrel to throw the haggis improbable distances. Events occur annually at highland games and festivals across Scotland and the world, but you'll need a strong throwing arm, as the competition is stiff.

Haggis ingredients include a boiled sheep's stomach stuffed with its heart, liver, and lungs, as well as oatmeal, suet, onion, and spices.

AMEN!

R✝A✝D
REVEREND

English vicar Steven Young took to the ski slopes on May 1, 2019, to perform the first snowboarding church service in history.

The vicar's blessing commemorated the end of the European ski season and took place at Chill Factore, an indoor ski slope in Manchester, England. During the snow blessing, the Greater Manchester Rock Choir performed Beyoncé's "Halo" while Reverend Young boarded down the slope wearing his clerical collar and clutching a Bible. The vicar has raised nearly £1,500 ($1,910) this year to sponsor his attempt at snowboarding down each of the UK's six indoor ski slopes in just one day.

Egg Head

Erin Balogh of San Marcos, California, braided her 10-year-old daughter's hair into an egg-filled Easter basket! For those wanting to recreate the look, Balogh suggests gathering a few supplies: hair clips, hair ties, and a headband, plus decorations like miniature Easter eggs, ribbons, and crinkle paper. Balogh's YouTube channel contains instructional videos for other bizarre updos, too, like donut hair with real pink frosting and sprinkles.

ENDURANCE TEST

On August 4, 2018, double amputee Matthew "Bushy" McKelvey, from Pietermaritzburg, South Africa, rode 1,712 mi (2,740 km) on a motorcycle in 24 hours at the Hakskeen Pan race track. He lost his right leg in 1999 and his left leg in 2008, both in biking accidents.

SKATER GIRL

Yanise Ho, from Toronto, Ontario, Canada, traveled coast to coast across the United States on rollerblades—a seven-month solo trip of 3,850 mi (6,160 km). She set off from Miami, Florida, and skated all the way to Portland, Oregon, by November 2018, even though she had never skated on rollerblades until 2016. She carried no money with her and relied on the kindness of strangers to give her food and shelter every night.

151,409

The number of times Hijiki Ikuyama from Japan skipped rope in 24 hours, averaging 105 skips every minute.

VETERAN IRONMAN

Japan's Hiromu Inada completed the 2018 Ironman World Championships in Kona, Hawaii, at age 85. He finished the 2.4-mi (3.8-km) swim, the 112-mi (180-km) bike ride, and the 26.2-mi (42-km) marathon with more than six minutes to spare before the 17-hour cutoff time.

ROAD TRIP

Mikah Meyer has visited all 419 U.S. National Park Service sites. He set off on April 29, 2016, at the Washington Monument and finished back in Washington, D.C., at the Lincoln Memorial, exactly three years later. He drove 75,000 mi (120,000 km) by van and also traveled by train, airplane, and boat to reach the more distant destinations. His favorite park was the remote Dinosaur National Monument on the border of Utah and Colorado, which is about three hours from the nearest interstate highway.

This particular bike is 8.5 ft (2.4 m) high but can be extended to 10.2 ft (3.1 m) tall!

Riding High

Rajeev Kumar has a passion for designing and riding colossal bikes that range from 8 to 13 ft (2.4 to 4 m) tall. Also known as Johny, Kumar pedals his towering creations across India to raise awareness about pollution and the health of the planet. In one of his most well-known stunts, he rode 16 hours from Chandigarh to Delhi on a cycle measuring 7.5 ft (2.3 m) tall. Kumar once built a bike that was 13 ft (4 m) tall, but the police forbade him from riding it in his hometown!

Ripley's Exhibit
Cat. No. 173119

Matchstick Dodge Charger

A 2/3-size scale model of the iconic *Fast & Furious*
Dodge Charger made entirely out of matchsticks.
Created by Patrick Acton.

Ripley's Exhibit
Cat. No. 169097

Matchstick Minas Tirith

A recreation of Minas Tirith made famous by
J. R. R. Tolkien's *The Lord of the Rings*, built
out of more than 420,000 matchsticks, 24,000
domino-sized wooden blocks, and 10 gal (38 l) of
wood glue. Created by Patrick Acton.

inside the vault

Ripley's Exhibit
Cat. No. 169535

Matchstick ISS
Model of a portion of the
International Space Station (ISS)
built entirely out of matchsticks.
Created by Patrick Acton.

POSTCARD SWEATERS

Instead of buying souvenirs from the places he visits, Sam Barsky of Baltimore, Maryland, knits postcard sweaters and then wears them on location for epic photoshoots.

From Niagara Falls to the Canary Islands, Barsky's got a sweater for just about every iconic spot on the globe—*and* a photo of him wearing them at each location. He started knitting 17 years ago after a learning disability and neurological disorder prevented him from finishing nursing school. A local yarn shop agreed to teach him the craft if he promised to buy all of his yarn there. He's kept his promise and then some in his quest to knit the world.

Reptiles

Red Rock Canyon

Owls

Sweater of Sweaters

Stonehenge

DAILY SWIM

Peter Hancock, from New South Wales, Australia, has not missed a daily swim for more than 2,000 days. He has swum outdoors regularly for more than 20 years and even swims with icebergs off the coast of New Zealand, braving water temperatures of less than 35°F (2°C).

JUMP POT

Theo "Blood Shark" Mihellis, a 14-year-old from Dormont, Pennsylvania, potted a billiard ball on a pool table by shooting it over a bar that was 16 in (40 cm) high. He pulled off the trick shot, called a jump pot, on his first attempt and had only been playing for seven months.

Fred Reissman, of Mooresville, North Carolina, collected 228 four-leaf clovers in just under two hours.

SCHOOL WRESTLER

Born with a rare muscle weakness that severely affects his arms, Devin McLane, from Stevensville, Montana, has learned to use his feet to write, eat, cook, and do archery. He is even a member of his school wrestling team, where he has learned to wrestle without using his arms.

HIPPO DANGER

Martin Hobbs from South Africa spent 54 days swimming the entire 361-mi (578-km) length of Lake Malawi, which is home to deadly hippos and crocodiles. He took up swimming in 2013 after a back injury ended his off-road biking and marathon running careers.

BEARD BROS

Just when you thought Portland couldn't get any weirder, two Oregon artists have upped the ante with The Gay Beards.

Childhood best friends Brian and Jonathan have always celebrated creativity. But the artistic impulse coalesced for both men after they started growing facial hair in 2014. That's when a friend convinced them to put a few flowers in their beards and pose for photos. After seeing their popularity with friends and family, the duo was on a mission to spread love and laughter. The Gay Beards were born! Today, they fearlessly push social constructs and decorate their facial hair with anything from flowers to food, glitter, and even cupcake sprinkles.

Lumber Laptops

A family of computer specialists in Peru recently released a sustainable wooden laptop designed to last for 10 to 15 years. The Carrascos created this sturdy, affordable technology to bring the benefits of the internet to some of the most remote parts of their nation. Lightweight and ultraportable, the laptop costs only $235.

GUITAR HEROES

The band Aerosmith has earned more money from the video game *Guitar Hero* than from any of its albums.

ADVANCED COPY

President Obama received an advanced copy of season four of the TV show *Game of Thrones* because he was unable to fit the TV screenings into his busy work schedule.

BUTT PICTURE

Swiss artist Jinks Kunst spent three years collecting over 23,000 discarded cigarette butts off the streets and then used them to create a portrait of French singer and actor Serge Gainsbourg.

EXTENSIVE PLAYTIME

The video game *Call of Duty* was only released in 2003, but with more than 25 billion hours (2.85 million years) of total game playtime, people have already played it for longer than human existence.

ALBUM TITLE

English musician George Ezra's 2018 album *Staying at Tamara's* was named after his host at an Airbnb in Barcelona, Spain, with whom he has kept in touch.

CRACKER MOSAIC

A 43-ft-long (13-m), 30-ft-wide (9-m) mosaic reproduction of the *Mona Lisa* was constructed in Soka, Japan, from 24,000 rice crackers. To achieve different colors, the crackers were coated with a variety of liquids, including soy sauce and green tea.

UK mosaic artist Ed Chapman made portraits of 10 famous people—including scientist Sir Isaac Newton, Robin Hood, and film director Richard Attenborough—out of 3,000 used train tickets.

FITNESS TRAINING

American actress Brie Larson trained for nine months to play Captain Marvel, and by the end she could deadlift 225 lb (102 kg) and also push a 5,000-lb (2,270-kg) Jeep, with a full tank of gas and a driver, uphill for a whole minute.

SNOWNA LISA

In February 2019, Robert Greenfield used a shovel to make a large portrait of the *Mona Lisa* from the snow in the backyard of his home in Toronto, Ontario, Canada.

SMALL AUDIENCE

For 40 years, Deke Duncan, from Stevenage, England, operated a radio station from his garden shed, broadcasting to an audience of only one—his wife.

LOST PROPERTY

The Royal Philharmonic Orchestra performed a concert at London's St. Pancras International Station using "instruments" that had been left behind on trains—including a surfboard, harp, drum, guitar, and an inflatable cactus.

NAME CHECK

Gwen Stefani was named after Gwen Meighen, the flight attendant in Arthur Hailey's 1968 novel *Airport*, and her middle name, Renée, is thought to come from The Four Tops' 1968 hit "Walk Away Renée."

DAIRY UPBRINGING

John Cleese's father's surname was originally Cheese. Cleese grew up in Somerset, England, 10 mi (16 km) from Cheddar, and his best friend at school was Barney Butter.

REARRANGED

New Jersey artist Adam Hillman creates brilliant rainbow-colored art pieces using everyday objects such as lollipops and sticky notes.

His Zen-like patterns emphasize the vibrant colors of objects we take for granted in everyday life, from Tic Tacs to toothpicks to Froot Loops. He calls his particular art style "Object Arranging," and it requires skills from multiple disciplines, including painting, photography, and sculpture.

LARGEST
BUDDHA
IN THE
WORLD!

BIG BUDDHA

The Leshan Giant Buddha measures 233 ft (71 m) tall, 79 ft (24 m) wide at its shoulders, and took more than 90 years to carve.

With construction starting in 713 AD during the Tang Dynasty, the Buddha's symmetrical posture is positively massive! Its fingers measure 27 ft (8.3 m) long, and it boasts a 36-ft-long (11-m) foot that can fit more than 100 people. But it's the Buddha's carefully carved features that are so captivating. The statue bears a broad smile, and his hair contains 1,021 intricately coiled buns.

The Buddha has 23-ft-long (7-m) ears, capable of holding two people inside.

MY LITTLE PONY

From intricate clips that commemorate World War I to styles that celebrate Native Americans, this "horse barber" has elevated equine haircuts to an art form.

A genuine pony-Picasso, British entrepreneur Melody Hames has found a unique way to combine her love of horses with her background in graphic design. She crafts one-of-a-kind horse clips custom-tailored to each of her clientele and their owner's unique requests. Her standout clips include a whimsical *Alice in Wonderland*–themed tea party and a festive "gingerbread horse" clip.

Bird Bloom

While flowers have been known to resemble everything from butterflies to rabbit ears, nothing comes close to the imitation job done by the green birdflower (*Crotalaria cunninghamii*). Found primarily in unstable sand dunes of northern Australia, the plant produces flowers shaped just like miniature hummingbirds.

Darwilla

A new metal sculpture at Shrewsbury's Darwin Centre in the UK has caused quite a stir with its hybrid depiction of Charles Darwin as a big, hairy gorilla. Crafted by artist Luke Kite, the sculpture celebrates the famous English naturalist whose discovery of natural selection gave further credence to the theory of evolution. Titled *Gorilla Apocalypse*, the work is part of an initiative to encourage creative excellence in rural Great Britain.

PUPPY SNATCH

A puppy named Latte was snatched by an owl from a Scottsdale, Arizona, backyard and carried off before being dropped on a golf course. She was found dehydrated and suffering from puncture wounds, but she made a full recovery.

INCREDIBLE ESCAPE

After being hit by a car at 60 mph (96 kmph) in Adelaide Hills, Australia, a sulfur-crested cockatoo was wedged in the vehicle's front grille for two hours, but when the bird was eventually cut free, it was found to be unharmed.

The brown thrasher, a North American bird, has a repertoire of more than 3,000 different sounds.

FALLING STARLINGS

On September 14, 2018, 42 dead or dying European starlings fell from the sky head-first and landed around Kevin Beech's car on the highway south of Vancouver, British Columbia, Canada.

LONELY DUCK

In 2018, there were 1,624 humans on the remote Pacific island of Niue but only one duck—a solitary male mallard named Trevor. The bird's unexpected arrival prompted the island's residents to bring him food and add water to the puddle where he lived, and he soon became a tourist attraction.

WORM INFECTION

Due to a parasitic worm infection, Tawheeda Jan, from Jammu and Kashmir state, India, has feet that are three times bigger than normal, leaving her unable to wear shoes. She was born with the condition known as elephantiasis and has had eight of her toes removed in an attempt to stop her feet from growing.

EYEBALL POPPED

In a game against Cairns Taipans in Auckland, New Zealand, Akil Mitchell, an American Panamanian basketball player representing the New Zealand Breakers, had his left eyeball pop out of its socket as he challenged for a rebound. Happily, doctors were able to pop it back into place and he regained his vision.

NUCLEAR CODE

For 15 years during the Cold War, from 1962 to 1977, the United States nuclear launch code was 00000000. The simple code was chosen to make it as quick and easy as possible to launch the weapons.

Burning Rubber

The Autoped, a personal transport system originally developed in 1915, was an early version of today's scooters. This scooter was well ahead of its time, with its motorized engine that topped out at 20 mph (32 kmph). The Autoped was equipped with headlights and taillights, a horn, and even included a toolbox!

MACHINE MADNESS

This isn't your average vending machine! Taylor Valdés of Portland, Oregon, created these wacky vending machines to showcase local artists.

Taylor was initially inspired by unconventional vending machines she'd seen in South Korea, as well as the 24-hour Church of Elvis. The result? Old, glittery machines filled with an eclectic array of items. You'll find everything from hangover cures to local artwork, junk drawer finds to toy animals paired with handwritten fortunes. Fast-forward six years and The Venderia has worked with hundreds of local makers and artists. Together, they constantly revamp their collection of bizarre and strange vending machine–friendly items.

HELTER SKELTER

BACKSLIDING BISHOP!

The Norwich Cathedral in Norfolk, England, recently saw the installation of a 55-ft-tall (16.8-m) helter skelter fairground ride inside its nave.

Constructing the slide required 19 hours of labor and the assembly of more than 1,000 pieces, using 500 nuts and bolts and 2,000 lights. The goal of the ride? To get people thinking and talking about faith in new ways as a part of the "Seeing It Differently" initiative.

GRAINY IMAGES

These meticulously crafted portraits are made by pouring and shaping colorful sand inside jars, glasses, and fishbowls!

What do you get the person who has everything? An intricate portrait handcrafted solely from colored sand! The masterminds behind the Instagram account @FallingInSand use extremely fine, grade A sand imported from Jordan. Before beginning a piece, the sand gets washed, graded, purified, and dyed with permanent colors. Then, through the patience, skill, and steady hand of the artist, a one-of-a-kind artwork emerges.

LIGHTS ON!

LIGHTS OFF!

GLOWS IN THE DARK!

LOVE 100%

FINAL PIECE!

ON POINTE

Poppy Fairbairn can dance ballet on the shoulders of her partner, Zion Martyn!

The couple performs in Australia under the name Zion & Poppy and are the only ones in their country able to achieve these maneuvers, known as *pointe adagio*. Despite the slow and deliberate movements that come with dancing adagio, their performance is an exhilarating one thanks to the intense concentration and balance required on both Zion and Poppy's parts.

To dance *en pointe* in ballet, the dancer must be balanced on the tips of his or her toes.

Ballin'

Finley the golden retriever, aka @finnyboymolloy, can hold multiple tennis balls in his mouth at once! The Canandaigua, New York, pup is naturally talented, having surprised his owners, Cheri and Rob Molloy, when he was just two years old by picking up four tennis balls in his mouth. Nowadays, Finley can pick up six—talk about a mouthful!

DO YA WANNA FETCH?

SWALLOWED SPOON

A woman in Shenzen, China, accidentally swallowed a 5-in-long (12.7-cm) stainless steel spoon while using it to dislodge a fish bone that was stuck in her throat. She did not go to the hospital to report the accident until four days later because she was not experiencing any stomach pain. Surgeons managed to remove the spoon.

LEOPARD EXERCISE

The nearly 70-year-old Chinese grandfather Mi Youren performs a daily public fitness routine in city parks and squares based on the movements of a leopard. To look the part, he wears a full leopard costume, complete with tail and pointy ears.

WRONG THOMAS

Plans to honor French architect Jean-François Thomas de Thomon with a statue in St. Petersburg, Russia, ended in embarrassment when seven years later it was revealed that sculptor Alexander Taratynov had mistakenly depicted Thomas Thomson, a 19th-century Scottish chemist who had no connection with the city.

Accio Blocks!

A team known as the Floo Network spent two years meticulously recreating the world of Harry Potter in Minecraft! They included details any Harry Potter fan would recognize, such as moving staircases and floating candles. Players can download the map and play as a Hogwarts student, doing everything from attending classes, casting spells, and flying on broomsticks to exploring the school grounds—including the Chamber of Secrets!

HOGWARTS CASTLE

GREAT HALL

WEAR YOUR HEART ON YOUR SHELL

With plenty of TLC, an albino turtle with a rare condition that leaves her heart exposed to the world continues to thrive and personify "hope."

From her tiny size to her exposed heart, everything about Hope, the albino pinkbelly sideneck turtle, proves both fragile and inspiring. She suffers from a condition so rare that veterinarians have never seen it before in turtles. Known as ectopia cordis, it occurs in six in every million human births. Yet Hope's owner, Mike Aquilina of New Jersey, has helped her flourish despite the odds.

SPOTTED!

As photographer Rahul Sachdev recently found out while visiting the Maasai Mara in Kenya, zebras of a different stripe (or spot) *do* stick together!

Sachdev captured a unique spotted pattern on a zebra foal that appears to be pseudo-melanistic. This genetic anomaly results in unique pigmentation with telltale enlarged stripes or dark spots covering areas of the body. In this case, the condition has given the foal a dappled appearance. While hereditary, the condition can skip generations and is often passed on by individuals with no visible signs of the condition.

Hungry Hungry Catfish

The Wels catfish of the Tarm River, France, have devised an ingenious way to secure a meal: picking off fat pigeons who bathe along the river's banks. But only a select few can pull it off. The hungry catfish must be small enough to sneak up on the pigeons in shallow water, yet strong enough to beach themselves, grab a bird, and pull it back into the water. Ironically, the most successful pigeon hunters quickly outgrow the shallow waters, making it impossible for them to sneak up on future birds.

SNACK ATTACK!

Ripley's Exhibit

Cat. No. 173958

The Starry Night Lint Art

Vincent van Gogh's *The Starry Night* painting composed entirely from lint. Created by Laura Bell.

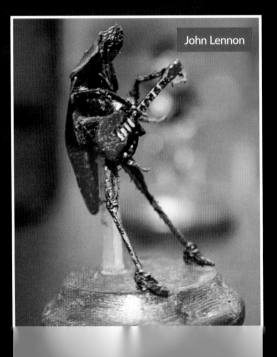

John Lennon

Jimi Hendrix

Ripley's Exhibit

Cat. No. 174436,

Cockroach Rockers

Miniature fig of classic roc musicians cre with preserv cockroaches. are John Le Jimi Hendri

Ripley's Exhibit

Cat. No. 168586

Computer Keyboard Art

This piece contains 5,981 computer keyboard keys — approximately 70 keyboards' worth — and took 190 hours to complete. Hidden in the keys are several NASA and space-related words, including "Endeavor," "NASA," "thrust," "payload," and "Atlantis." Created by Doug Powell.

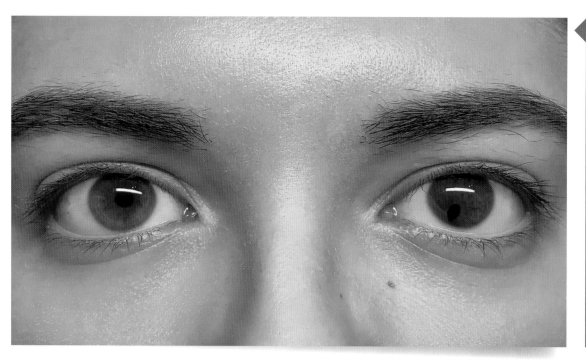

Positive Pupil

Pernilla Beatrice, a law student from Rome, has learned to overcome childhood bullying and embrace her rare eye abnormality, known as corectopia, by posting photos on social media. Beatrice is comforted by the supportive comments she's received for her eye images, which show a smaller-than-usual, irregularly shaped pupil located near the bottom of her left eye's iris.

FIRST CIRCUMNAVIGATION
In 2018, Ross Edgley, from Grantham, England, became the first person to swim 1,780 mi (2,848 km) around the entire coast of Great Britain. It took him 155 days, swimming up to 12 hours a day, and during that time he never once set foot on dry land. He kept up his strength by eating more than 500 bananas, but the constant exposure of salt water to his face caused pieces of his tongue to fall off.

WIRE STUNT
High-wire stuntman Freddy Nock spent eight and a half hours sitting on a chair that was balanced on a tightrope at a shopping mall in Ebikon, Switzerland .

NOSE BLOW
Tang Feihu, from Kaiyang, China, took only two and a half minutes to inflate 12 car tires simultaneously by blowing through a tube attached to his nostril.

JENGA GAME
Using huge loading machines and excavators, U.S. construction equipment manufacturer Caterpillar Inc. created a game of Jenga featuring 27 pine beams, each weighing around 600 lb (272 kg). Each beam measured 8 ft (2.4 m) long, 2.7 ft (0.8 m) wide, and 1.3 ft (0.4 m) high. The game went on for 28 hours and ended up with 13 layers, for a total height of about 20 ft (6 m).

Hoof Patrol

Mounted police on the Brazilian island of Marajo have given the term "Buffalo Soldiers" a new meaning by spurning horses in favor of 1,000-lb (454-kg) water buffalo. Marajo contains 450,000 of these creatures, with many domesticated for agricultural purposes. But it's their use as the steeds of local law enforcement that draws, by far, the most attention.

JUST KIDNEYING!

A 56-year-old man with a genetic disorder in India recently had a 16.3-lb (7.4-kg) kidney removed— possibly the world's largest.

Surgeons who performed the operation were astounded by the size of the cyst-covered organ. A healthy adult's kidney typically weighs less than 0.3 lb (0.2 kg)! This monstrosity was nearly 7 lb (3.2 kg) heavier than the former record-holder, a 9.3-lb (4.3-kg) specimen removed from a patient in Dubai with polycystic kidney disease.

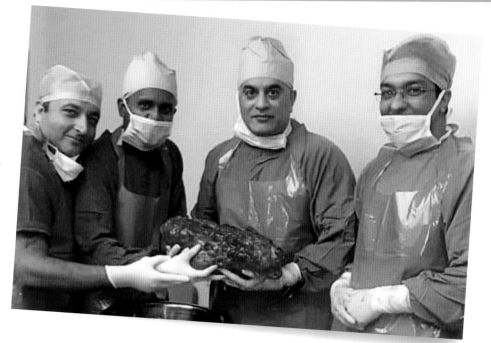

TACTILE
MASTERPIECE

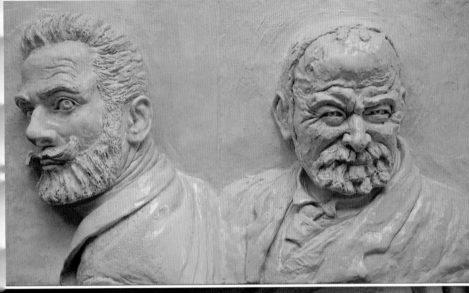

These sculptures are 3D replicas of famous classic paintings that allow the blind to experience the artistry!

French artist Quitterie Ithurbide has developed a remarkable way to translate famous artworks into bas-relief sculptures that blind people can interpret. The result? Famous masterpieces are now, quite literally, at their fingertips. From Van Gogh to Degas, Berthe Morisot to Munch, Ithurbide has opened up a whole new world of art to the visually impaired through her touchable sculptures.

Ithurbide's sculptures are not just for the blind; sighted people have reported seeing things in her recreations that they had never noticed in the original paintings.

TICKLED P•I•N•K

Photographer Kristian Laine was diving off the coast of Australia when a confusing sight made him think his camera equipment was on the fritz—a pink manta ray!

Inspector Clouseau, as he is called (a reference to the detective character in *Pink Panther*), is the world's only known pink manta ray. First spotted in 2015, the 11-ft (3.5-m) manta has since been studied to find out what makes his complexion so rosy. Stress, infection, and a red-filled diet (à la flamingos) were ruled out via biopsy, so now scientists believe Clouseau exhibits a genetic mutation that affects his pigmentation, much like albinism.

PINOCCHIO FROG

Male Indonesian tree frogs have been hopping around the jungle sporting a spiky nose appendage, and scientists didn't know about it until 2008. Herpetologist Paul Oliver was deep in the Foja Mountains taking shelter from a deluge when he spotted a little specimen casually sitting on a bag of rice. It's since been named the Pinocchio frog for obvious reasons. Although no one "nose" what the spike is for, it can interestingly droop or stick out straight.

NEW MANTIS

A recent expedition to the Brazilian rainforest discovered at least five new species of mantises. They included a previously undiscovered form of unicorn mantis, with a prominent single horn on its head and striking red limbs.

HOLDING HANDS

Sea otters hold hands while they are asleep on the ocean surface to keep them from drifting apart. While eating, sleeping, and resting, they float in groups called rafts, and a single raft can have hundreds of otters.

DEADLY OCTOPUS

Found in oceans from Japan to Australia, the blue-ringed octopus measures only around 5 in (12.5 cm) long, but its painless bite contains enough venom to kill 26 adult humans within minutes.

CLAM FEAST

Walruses weigh almost 3,700 lb (1,700 kg) and can eat up to 4,000 clams in one feed. Despite their bulk, they are capable of swimming at over 20 mph (32 kmph). They use their 3-ft-long (0.9-m) tusks to break through ice and also to help lift themselves out of the water and onto the ice.

REJUVENATING POOP

Aging fish are likely to live for up to 40 percent longer if they eat the poop of younger fish. Consuming the microbes in the feces of young fish rejuvenates them and makes them healthier.

BOWLING PARROT

Scout the Senegal parrot of Gloucestershire, England, can fetch, wave, and roll over, as well as skateboard and bowl. Owner Sara Hannant started training Scout shortly after she brought her home as a chick, and now the bird entertains almost 9,000 followers on the Instagram: @p_isforparrot.

LEECH FEAST

Mount Kinabalu in Borneo is home to a leech that doesn't suck blood. Instead, the Kinabalu giant red leech (*Mimobdella buettikoferi*) feeds on Kinabalu giant earthworms (*Pheretima darnleiensis*), sucking up its defenseless prey whole. The disturbing phenomenon was captured for the first time in 2014. The Kinabalu giant red leech can grow to a length of more than 19 in (50 cm).

HIDDEN PYRAMID

Built around 300 BC, the Great Pyramid of Cholula in Mexico measures 1,480 × 1,480 ft (451 × 451 m), with its base being four times larger than that of Egypt's Great Pyramid of Giza and nearly twice the volume!

A Spanish army led by Hernán Cortéz invaded Cholula in 1519 but did not notice the massive structure, as it was hidden beneath layers of soil and vegetation. The Spaniards settled in the area and unwittingly built a church atop of what they thought was a large hill, which is still there. Today, a small part of the Great Pyramid of Cholula has been excavated and can be explored via tunnels. Believe it or not, the pyramid, known locally as Tlachihualtepetl, is the largest monument ever constructed!

The Great Pyramid of Cholula as it is today, covered in soil and topped with a church.

An artist's rendition of what the Great Pyramid of Cholula looked like in its heyday thousands of years ago.

PYRAMIDS OF THE WORLD

Pyramids appear all over the world, created by ancient civilizations who had no knowledge of each other. But this isn't the work of some supernatural or alien being—the pyramid shape just happens to be an efficient way to build large monuments, and the architects of these ancient civilizations knew that. Here are just a few impressive pyramids from around the globe.

Great Pyramid of Giza
The Great Pyramid of Giza in Egypt is probably the most famous pyramid in the world. Also known as the Pyramid of Khufu, it was built around 2560 BC and held the title of tallest man-made structure for more than 3,800 years!

Ziggurat of Ur
The Sumerian Ziggurat of Ur in Iraq was built for King Ur-Nammu in the mid-2000s BC and once boasted three stories of terraced brick connected by staircases and crowned by a shrine to the moon god.

Pyramid of Cestius
Sticking out like a sore thumb is the 119-ft-tall (36-m) Pyramid of Cestius in Rome, Italy. Originally built for a Roman senator between 18 and 12 BC, the structure sits between two ancient roads, with one half sitting in a cemetery.

Pyramid of the Sun
The central Mexican city of Teotihuacan once measured 8 sq mi (21 sq km), punctuated by several pyramids, including the 760-ft-wide (231.6-m), five-stepped Pyramid of the Sun.

Nubian Pyramids
Hundreds of small, narrow Nubian pyramids line the sands of modern-day Sudan, a testament to the ancient Kushite civilization, which ruled the region from approximately 2450 BC to 350 AD.

GUITARCODE SCANNER

When not making robots, James Bruton of Southampton, England, assembles unlikely components, including barcodes, to craft musical instruments.

Bruton's latest creation, the Barcode Guitar, relies on a barcode scanner to play various notes. These notes, in turn, get manipulated using arcade controls. Each barcode includes ASCII values. When scanned, their equivalent integers get sent to an external MIDI device, generating each sound. The result is synthetic music to our ears.

Bomb Garden

On September 20, 1940, a Nazi airplane pilot bombed London during the Blitz. His target? Westminster Cathedral. Fortunately, the bomb missed, creating a large crater between Morphet Terrace and the cathedral choir instead. Seizing the opportunity, Mr. Hayes, the cathedral's caretaker, transformed the hole into a "victory garden."

TREE FAN
Resistencia Sport Club, a Paraguayan soccer team, has made a tree growing through a hole in the stands of its La Chacharita stadium an official supporter. The 100-year-old, 66-ft-tall (20-m) tree has its own team membership card and jersey.

HOME STOLEN
Meghan Panu's 20-ft-long (6-m) mobile home was stolen from its location in St. Louis, Missouri, and found a few days later 30 mi (48 km) away in House Springs.

A wheelchair that once belonged to English scientist Stephen Hawking sold for about $387,000 in 2018.

SNAP DECISION
When Brandon Keith Hatfield broke into the St. Augustine Alligator Farm Zoological Park in Florida, he was promptly bitten on the foot by a 9-ft-long (2.7-m) reptile, coincidentally while he was wearing Crocs shoes!

NAKED PASSENGER
A naked man who tried to board an airplane at Domodedovo Airport in Moscow, Russia, claimed that clothing made him less aerodynamic.

Dead Sea Tree

A lifeless body of water located between Jordan and Israel, the Dead Sea contains about ten times the salt content of the ocean. Yet, perched atop a white-salt island floating amid the Dead Sea is a tree. Local artist Amiram Dora planted the tree there as an art installation, and he paddleboards out daily to pack nutrient-rich mud around its root base.

GHOST CHURCH

Forty years ago, parishioners abandoned a church in the Czech Republic, fearing paranormal activity. Now, ghostly sculptures are bringing visitors back.

Consecrated in 1352, Kostel svatého Jiří (St. George's Church) sat in ruins by 1968. Its painful history includes WWII-era Nazi occupation and a string of seemingly paranormal events, including fires and a falling roof, that spooked parishioners into abandoning it. But in 2012, an unlikely event saved the church from further decay. Artist Jakub Hadrava placed 30 life-sized casts of humans draped in white throughout the church. Today, visitors flock from all over the world to photograph and sit amid the phantom congregation.

800,000

The number of members at Yoido Full Gospel Church in Seoul, South Korea, representing one person in every 12 in the city. A total of more than 80,000 people regularly attend the seven Sunday services, while up to 150,000 more watch on TV screens in overflow chapels.

NAME CHANGE
The town of DISH, Texas, was originally named Clark until 2005, when the community agreed to a new name as part of an agreement with a satellite TV company. In return, all 200 residents received free TV service for 10 years and a free digital video recorder.

STEEP RAILWAY
The Scenic Railway in Australia's Blue Mountains has a 52-degree (128 percent) incline, making it one-and-a-half times steeper than a ski jump.

SHEEP RUN
In response to Spain's famous Running of the Bulls festival, the New Zealand town of Te Kuiti stages an annual Running of the Sheep event, featuring hundreds of sheep running through the streets.

CITY RAINFOREST
Panama City has a rainforest within its city limits. Overlooking the Panama Canal, the Gamboa Rainforest is home to caymans, crocodiles, monkeys, and several hundred bird species but is located just 15 mi (25 km) from the heart of the city.

UNDERGROUND HOTEL
The Intercontinental Shanghai Wonderland Hotel in China has only two stories aboveground but 15 more stories that plunge 289 ft (88 m) belowground. Built into the side of an old quarry, the 336-room, five-star "groundscraper" even has underwater suites.

VAST COUNTY
Brewster County, Texas, covers an area of 6,192 sq mi (16,037 sq km), making it two-and-a-half times larger than the entire state of Delaware.

TO THE BEAT

Despite being deaf and thus unable to hear the music, the members of this Chinese dance troupe are world-renowned for their lyrical classical ballet, Chinese folk music, and Latin dance routines.

Dancing at the professional level requires years of training, extreme self-discipline, and a thorough sensitivity to music, yet the deaf performers of the China Disabled People's Performing Arts Troupe have overcome the odds to create perfect numbers. They internalize beats stamped out for them on the floor of the practice studio and rely on strategically placed "conductors" during their performances. Their awe-inspiring routines include the clocklike precision of the Thousand Hand Dance, shown here.

Ripley's Exhibit

Cat. No. 11914

Elephant Jaw

Elephant jaw complete with teeth.

Front view

inside the vault

Ripley's Exhibit
Cat. No. 23688

Inuit
Spirit Mask

Alaskan Inuit spirit
mask created from a
whale vertebra using
the spinal opening
as a mouth. The eyes
and teeth are walrus
ivory. The hair is
polar bear fur.

Ripley's Exhibit
Cat. No. 22023

Cricket Cage

Chinese cricket cage
made from bone.

FIVE SPIDERS ON HIS FACE!

LEGO ARM

Born with a rare genetic condition that left him without a right forearm, 19-year-old David Aguilar, a bioengineering student in Barcelona, Spain, built a prosthetic arm out of LEGO bricks. His LEGO arm, made from a crane set, contains small electric motors to help the elbows and hands function like a real limb. He built his first basic artificial arm when he was just nine.

DOUBLE DIPLOMA

In 2019, 17-year-old Braxton Moral graduated from Harvard just 11 days after leaving high school. On May 19, he received his diploma from Ulysses High School, Kansas, but because he had also been studying part-time for fun with Harvard for six years, on May 30 he was able to collect his undergraduate degree from Harvard Extension School.

UNICYCLE TOUR

Ed Pratt, from Somerset, England, rode a 36-in-high (0.9-m) unicycle around the world. His 18,000-mi (29,000-km) unsupported journey took him three years and four months but got off to a bad start when, on his very first day, he was only able to cover 7 mi (11.3 km) after breaking his bag's zipper while trying to cram egg sandwiches inside.

BUGGING OUT!

While the thought of holding insects and arachnids may make most people's skin crawl, bug enthusiast Kelvin Wiley goes to lip-smacking measures to prove that these creatures are harmless.

Kelvin began as a fearless kid who loved to play with bugs and let them crawl on his arms and legs. He has spent a lifetime cultivating his fear response by getting more adventurous with the types of bugs he collects and where he lets them roam. That's right—this insect aficionado gets up close and personal with his collection by letting them crawl on his head and by placing them in his mouth!

He began collecting and breeding insects, arachnids, and arthropods in 2014, purchasing many of them from online sources or by going outside and picking them up himself. He houses these not-so-creepy crawlies in temperature-controlled enclosures in the basement of his home. Though Kelvin doesn't want to become an entomologist, he hopes to share his knowledge through social media to educate people about his unique friends.

HEAD SMASH

Mohammad Rashid Naseem, a martial artist from Pakistan, cracked open 247 walnuts with his head in one minute. The nuts were arranged in lines, and as Naseem began headbutting them in rapid succession, blood started to splatter onto the table, but he carried on regardless. He has also smashed 51 watermelons with his head in one minute.

ATLANTIC CROSSING

Lee Spencer, a former Royal Marine from Devon, England, rowed solo across the Atlantic Ocean from Portugal to French Guiana in South America in 60 days—despite having only one leg. He lost his right leg below the knee in a 2014 accident but still made the 3,800-mi (6,080-km) crossing 36 days faster than any able-bodied rower.

INCREDIBLE RECOVERY

Left in a coma and in the hospital for months after hitting his head on a fence post while skiing, teenager Ross Nesbitt, from East Renfrewshire, Scotland, was given only a 1 percent chance of making a full recovery. He had to learn how to walk, talk, and eat again—but just two years after the accident, he achieved seven "A" grades in his school exams.

MONUMENTAL ART

With 2,000 paper stickers and 400 volunteers, French artist Jean René transformed the Louvre pyramid into an amazing— albeit temporary— optical illusion.

René completed the art installation on March 29, 2019, to commemorate the 30th anniversary of the famous glass pyramid designed by American architect I. M. Pei. Measuring 183,000 sq ft (17,000 sq m), the grayscale image created an illusion of the pyramid extending below the ground into a massive, rocky pit. But the public didn't have long to contemplate René's work; within hours, the glue dried and every step taken by visitors tore the fragile paper, a final testament to René's meditation on impermanence.

INSTALLING THE OPTICAL ILLUSION!

Heart of the Paddy

A Chinese rice paddy recently transformed into art to commemorate the movie *Titanic*. Although more than 20 years have passed since the film's debut, the love story between *Titanic's* two main characters, Jack and Rose, lives on in the hearts of diehard fans—and one rice paddy in Shenyang, Liaoning Province in China. Using 3D and perspective technology and rice plants of various colors, workers painstakingly crafted the image, which is best appreciated from the air.

FAN FEED

SPOON FED

Spain's Marcos Ruiz Ceballos shared his amazing achievement with us: On August 7, 2016, he balanced 64 stainless-steel spoons simultaneously on his body. The "magnetic" event happened in Kashikojima, Japan, and although the stunt only lasted for five seconds, it took nearly four minutes for someone to place each spoon on his back and chest. He said, "I had to hold very still to keep all of the spoons in place."

STICKY SITUATION!

BAD TAXIDERMY

COWARDLY LION

Though he may not look like much, Leo, the lion of Gripsholm Castle in Mariefred, Sweden, is a preserved piece of (bad) taxidermy history.

Created in the 18th century, this wonky lion didn't start off with a twisty tongue. When gifted to King Frederick I from the Bey of Algiers in 1731, this lion was very much alive. Following its death, the king desired to have the hide stuffed and mounted. Unfortunately, it wasn't given to a taxidermist until several years after its death, meaning there was only a hide and bones to work with. Unfamiliar with what a lion actually looked like, the taxidermist most likely based this interpretation off of medieval heraldic lions.

MODEL

NAILED IT!

OVERSTUFFED →

Platypus Prank

Imagine being an 18th-century naturalist and getting your first look at the remains of an Australian platypus. A duck bill attached to a beaver body? As if! It was so crazy, it was widely considered a hoax. A mammal that laid eggs and secreted venom seemed even more outlandish. Because naturalists were so perplexed by the creature, it was treated like a joke when preserved, and many initial specimens are highly inaccurate.

Wrinkle Free

London's Horniman Museum is home to a walrus skin prepared in the late 1880s by a taxidermist who had never seen one. At the time, not many people had seen a living walrus, so the taxidermist was probably unaware that a walrus is a bulbous and (most importantly) wrinkly marine mammal. The taxidermist is likely to have treated the skin like a monstrous-sized seal, which were a more common sighting, filling the skin until smooth. Without its signature wrinkly body, the walrus was left looking like a rotund balloon with tusks!

Taxidermied walruses in a Los Angeles, California, museum put the over-inflated walrus to shame.

SWEATING CONDITION
Sophie Dwyer, from Houston, Texas, has hyperhidrosis, a condition that causes her to sweat 10 times more than the average person. She has to drink 1.5 gal (5.7 l) of water a day to replace the lost moisture. The excessive sweating soaks her clothes so much that in winter they sometimes freeze while she is wearing them.

SINGING SURVIVOR
Kay Longstaff, from Cheltenham, England, spent 10 hours in the Adriatic Sea off the coast of Croatia after plunging from the seventh deck of a cruise ship just before midnight. Found swimming the next morning, she credited yoga with keeping her fit enough to survive. She also sang to keep herself warm while in the water.

27-YEAR COMA
In 2018, Munira Abdulla from the United Arab Emirates finally woke up after spending 27 years in a coma—and was soon able to talk to her son. She had suffered a severe brain injury after being involved in a road accident in 1991, and doctors had given up all hope of her ever making a recovery.

SWIMMING KITES

Every May 5, Japanese kites shaped like carp, or koinobori, flutter in the wind to celebrate Children's Day, but the city of Hōfu has put a new twist on the tradition with kites that "swim" in the water.

Take one look at the Saba River in Yamaguchi Prefecture, and you'll be amazed by the colorful windsocks or kites gracing its waters each spring. A new twist on the koinobori that commemorate Children's Day, these underwater variants rival the size of small boats, filling the river with dramatic swathes of color. They perfectly typify carp, whose liveliness and courage have long been prized as admirable qualities to instill in children.

Auto-Bleeding

The ladybug has a very unusual defense mechanism to repel potential predators: auto-bleeding from their knees! Known as "reflex bleeding," ladybugs share this unique defensive tactic with a few other insects including the aptly named bloody-nosed beetle. How does auto-bleeding work? When ladybugs feel threatened, they secrete a bitter fluid through the joints in their exoskeletons containing hemolymph (their equivalent of blood) and noxious chemicals.

GOLD COIN

A rare British 1703 coin made using gold seized from a Spanish treasure ship sold for more than $1 million in 2019. Only 20 of the coins were ever minted from gold captured from a Spanish galleon at the Battle of Vigo Bay. The coins were struck to celebrate the British naval victory.

EEL SMUGGLERS

Two South Korean citizens were arrested at Zagreb airport, Croatia, while apparently trying to smuggle 252,000 live eels out of the country.

Shoemakers in medieval England used dog poop as part of the process of tanning the leather.

SELF-AMPUTATION

Kurt Kaser had to cut off his own leg with a pocket knife to free himself after he got caught in machinery on his farm in Pender, Nebraska. He was unloading corn when he accidentally stepped on the grain hopper opening, at which point his left leg was sucked in and mangled. Alone, unable to extricate himself, and with no phone in reach, he decided to take out his pocket knife and cut the leg off below the knee, somehow remaining conscious throughout the ordeal. He then crawled 150 ft (46 m) to reach a phone to call for help.

BIONIC COSPLAY

Actress Angel Giuffria and author Trace Wilson share a love of cosplay. Oh, and they also have high-tech prosthetic arms that they incorporate into their costumes!

Angel and Trace were both born missing an arm and actively seek out characters with limb differences to cosplay, like *Adventure Time*'s Finn the Human or Arsenal (aka Roy Harper) from the cartoon superhero show *Young Justice*. For them, limb difference representation in media is incredibly important, and they use their cosplays to show their love and support for characters who are more than their disabilities.

They use a variety of tools and materials, including foam, glue, fiberglass, and 3D printing, to integrate their prosthetics into their costumes and props.

Trace and Angel have myoelectric prosthetic arms, which are controlled by muscle movements in their forearms.

Stand Out

Mose the rescue dog stands out in a crowd—literally! He was born with only two limbs and taught himself to walk and run on his hind legs. His owners, Bo Lechangeur and Carrie Olivera, brought him to the Ripley's Believe It or Not! Odditorium in St. Augustine, Florida, for our Wild and Weird Halloween Extravaganza Pet Parade and Talent Show, where Mose won the coveted "Best Overall" category.

COW POSSE

Running from police officers in Sanford, Florida, suspect Jennifer Kaufman was finally arrested after being chased and cornered by a herd of 16 cows in a pasture.

SEVERED HAND

Police in Slovenia said a 21-year-old woman deliberately cut off her hand with a circular saw to collect nearly $450,000 in insurance money. She claimed she had been cutting tree branches when she severed her left hand just above the wrist, but officials became suspicious after it emerged that the family had recently signed contracts with five different insurance companies.

ROBOT DATING

A robotics association in Tokyo, Japan, staged a speed-dating event where shy humans sat in silence across a table from each other while miniature robots spoke on their behalf. The robots had been preprogrammed with relevant information about the people.

A 55-year-old woman from Manchester, England, asked a manufacturer to make her a designer handbag from the discarded skin of her amputated left leg.

MATCHING OUTFITS

Mother and son duo Pattharapol (aka "Peepy") and Lee Puengboonpra from Bangkok, Thailand, have worn matching outfits for more than six years.

ANGRY TWEETS

Dozens of angry tweets from Kansas City Chiefs fans intended for linebacker Dee Ford were sent instead to Dee Ford, a 47-year-old woman living 4,300 mi (6,920 km) away in Kent, England. The football player was not on Twitter.

CHOPPED FINGER

Pawan Kumar, from Uttar Pradesh, India, was so annoyed with himself after accidentally voting for the wrong candidate in the country's 2019 national election that he chopped off his index finger with a meat cleaver.

COSTLY OVERSIGHT

President Jimmy Carter once sent a jacket to the cleaners with the nuclear detonation codes still in the pocket.

BURNIN' DOWN THE BOAT

ew folkloric traditions contain as much combustible glee
s Taiwan's Burning of the Wang Yeh Boats, a tradition more
han 1,000 years in the making.

ne of Taiwan's top festivals, it spans eight days of exuberant celebration,
ulminating in a fiery spectacle on the beach. Events leading up to the cataclysmic
essel destruction include rituals inviting the gods to Earth to feast. Following
hese festivities, a boat is paraded through town before getting set alight. If you'd
ke to attend, keep in mind the phenomenon only happens once every three years.

The boat is surrounded by a massive pile of
Joss paper, or ghost money, which is burned
in order to be sent to people in the afterlife.

GOING TO **WASTE**

You can ski on the roof of a waste treatment plant in Copenhagen, Denmark!

Like other nations around the globe, Denmark has struggled with increased disposable waste in recent decades. One trash incineration plant in Copenhagen has developed a unique approach to the problem by constructing the first "green" ski runs. To do this, the waste plant lined its sloping 278-ft-tall (85-m) roof with an emerald substance known as neveplast that approximates the feel of skiing. The trash plant hopes to show residents that living near a waste treatment plant comes with unique perks!

HIT THE SLOPES!

Pooseum

Located in Yokohama, Japan, this bewildering museum focuses on everything "poo" with surprisingly pretty results. Just 30 minutes south of Tokyo by train, the Unko (Japanese word for "poo") Museum immerses you in a world of poop-themed play that's actually kind of cute. Instead of what you might expect from an institution dedicated to #2, the tourist hotspot focuses on a pastel-colored, soft-serve-shaped variety reminiscent of ice cream rather than the stinky alternative.

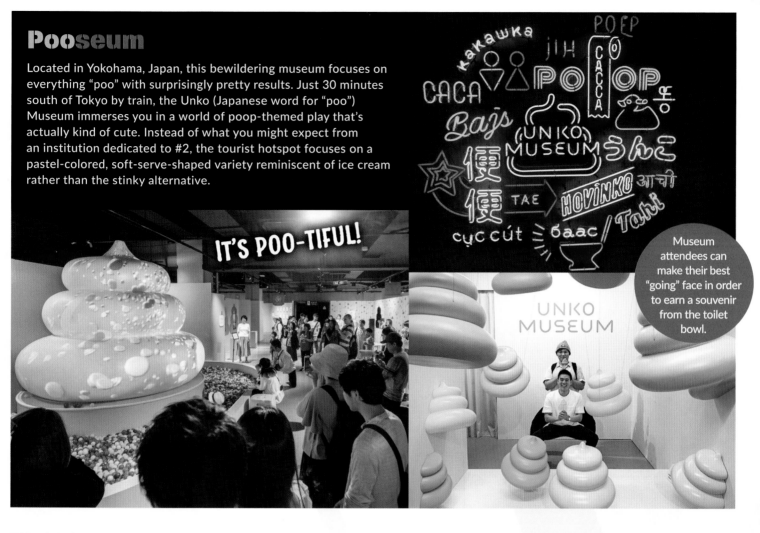

IT'S POO-TIFUL!

Museum attendees can make their best "going" face in order to earn a souvenir from the toilet bowl.

ELVIS SIGNALS

Friedberg, the German town where Elvis Presley served in the U.S. Army from 1958 to 1960, honored him in 2018 by putting a silhouette of him on pedestrian traffic signals. An image of Elvis standing at a microphone represented the red "Don't Walk" signal, and one of him performing a trademark dance move indicated the green "Walk" signal.

TREE FOUNTAIN

An old mulberry tree in Dinoša, Montenegro, turns into a natural water fountain whenever there is heavy rainfall. Since the tree stands in a pasture with numerous underground springs, the area floods during prolonged periods of rain. The pressure forces the water up the hollow trunk of the tree and out through a hole a few feet above the ground.

PAIN SAUCE

Developed by Steven Trim for his company in Kent, England, Scientific Steve's Venom Chilli Sauce mimics the bite of a venomous spider, the Trinidad chevron tarantula, which leaves its victims with temporary muscle spasms and burning pain. The sauce does not contain real tarantula toxin, but the makers created a synthetic version of the spider's venom in their laboratory.

450,000,000

The number of people that live within the danger zone of an active volcano— one in 10 of the world's population.

50-DAY QUAKE

A magnitude 5.8 earthquake hit Turkey near the city of Istanbul in the summer of 2016 and lasted for 50 days—but nobody felt it. The quake is known as a "slow slip" event, which involves very gradual movement along a fault and does not produce any shaking, leaving residents oblivious to what is taking place beneath their feet.

LONELY STATE

Of Montana's 56 counties, 45 have average populations of only six people or fewer per square mile.

SURGEON TATTOO

Nano Salguero, a grateful hospital patient from Alejo Ledesma, Argentina, got a large back tattoo showing the smiling face of Dr. Paul Lada, the surgeon who saved his life.

MOST NORTHERLY

The northernmost point of the Republic of Ireland (Inishtrahull) is further north than the northernmost point of Northern Ireland (Rathlin Island).

LONG CLIMB

If couples marry on picturesque Bled Island in Slovenia, the groom must carry the bride up 99 steps.

RIPLEY'S EXCLUSIVE

UNLEASHING
OUIJA ZILLA

Constructed of 99 individual sheets of plywood, clocking in at approximately 9,000 lb (4,082 kg), and measuring 3,168 sq ft (294 sq m), Ripley's Believe It or Not! would like to introduce you to Ouijazilla and its curious creator, Rick "Ormortis" Schreck!

Considered an object of the occult in mainstream media, talking boards have existed in one form or another since the birth of Modern Spiritualism. The most famous talking board, the brand name Ouija board, began as a simple board game first introduced by the Kennard Novelty Company in 1890.

Selling for $1.50 in 1891, "Ouija, the Wonderful Talking Board" was an allegedly magical device that answered questions via a wooden planchette—a teardrop-shaped indicator with a window in the middle—moving across a flat board featuring the letters of the alphabet; numbers 0 through 9; and the words "yes," "no," and "goodbye."

The idea was that two or more people would place their fingertips on the planchette, ask a question, and watch as an unseen force maneuvered the planchette over the letters to spell out a response. Believe it or not, the Ouija board was even considered a dating game!

Rick "Ormortis" Schreck, vice president of the Talking Board Historical Society and New Jersey–based tattoo artist, labored from June 2018 to October 2019 through wind, snow, rain, and extreme heat as the sole handyman on this monstrous project. Working with completely donated materials, Rick has poured his blood, sweat, and tears into this gargantuan board.

Q: WHERE DID THE IDEA FOR OUIJAZILLA COME FROM?

A: I started making normal-sized Ouija boards in 2004. But my idea for a larger one was that I wanted to paint a Ouija board on a football field, put a planchette on my truck, put the truck on the field, and put it in neutral to see where it would move. Then I talked about building the biggest physical board. Once I started constructing it, joking around, I said it's as large as Godzilla, so I started calling mine Ouijazilla.

Q: WHERE DID YOU CONSTRUCT OUIJAZILLA?

A: The little "dungeon" that I built Ouijazilla in is actually the garage attached to my tattoo shop. I worked on one piece at a time and watched horror VHS tapes on my little TV. The garage isn't climate controlled, so I worked through snow and over 100°F (37°C) heat.

Q: WHAT WAS YOUR DESIGN PROCESS?

A: I broke it down into small puzzle pieces. I took a 1998 glow-in-the-dark Parker Brothers Ouija board and drew a 1 × 2 in (2.5 × 5 cm) grid on it to map it out. I used an old projector I had from art school to enlarge each grid piece onto the 99 individual sheets of plywood so I could hand draw the stencils.

Q: DID YOU PUT TOGETHER THE ENTIRE BOARD AT ANY TIME DURING THIS PROCESS?

A: I didn't see Ouijazilla completely assembled until October 12, 2019. I had assembled two or three rows at a time in the parking lot, but I saw it in full the same time we unveiled it to the world.

Q: DID YOU EVER BUILD A LARGE BOARD PRIOR TO THE OUIJAZILLA PROJECT?

A: I built an 8 × 6 ft (2.4 × 1.8 m) board inspired by the TV show *Stranger Things* for Halloween one year. I rigged each letter and number with lights, connected each light to a keyboard, and hung it up outside my house. I would sit behind the window and wait for kids to ask it questions so the "board" could answer them.

Q: WHAT IS THE TALKING BOARD HISTORICAL SOCIETY?

A: The TBHS started out as a group of collectors who decided to band together and do good instead of always fighting over buying Ouija boards. We wanted to really uncover the history of these boards and share it with the world so it can be preserved.

OUIJAZILLA CREATOR RICK SCHRECK AND HIS FAMILY

A planchette is about the size of a human hand, but the Ouijazilla planchette could fit four people inside!

PARTS IN MOTION

Skateboarder Matt Tomasello of Boston, Massachusetts, showcases mind-boggling tricks on his custom-made, modified skateboards.

Taking inspiration from his friend's complex trick videos, Tomasello aims to make impossible maneuvers very much possible with decks that fold, unfold, rotate, and have trapdoors. Surrounded in his workshop by dozens of old skateboards, he sketches out his ideas before using power tools, home hardware, and bits and pieces from previous boards to construct new contraptions designed for creating unique moves.

Ripley's visited Matt to document the creation of this Frankensteined skateboard.

MIND-BENDING TRICKS!

Turf Tribute

Following the untimely passing of basketball legend Kobe Bryant in January 2020, a couple in Pleasanton, California, created a larger-than-life tribute in the grass of a local park. Kelli Pearson and Pete Davis used a GPS-equipped, lawnmower-like machine that "printed" the image by blowing blades of grass down in different directions to create light and dark areas. The image lasted for several days before the grass naturally stood back up.

"LA MORT" IS FRENCH FOR "THE DEATH."

Ripley's Exhibit
Cat. No. 19676

Death Omen Art

This ace of spades icon is actually a death omen. Acquired in 1972 by Ripley's.

The ace of spades was used by American soldiers as psychological warfare during the Vietnam War, which solidified its name as "The Death Card." The United States Playing Card Company even shipped thousands of 52-card ace of spades decks for free to troops in Vietnam after two soldiers requested them in February 1966.

Ripley's Exhibit
Cat. No. 5767

Death Money

Chinese death notes, also called "hell notes," were created by Chinese mourners who could not afford to bury real money with their dead relatives. This paper money was to be buried with the deceased so they could purchase goods and necessities in the afterlife.

Ripley's Exhibit
Cat. No. 166829

New Guinea Widow's Finger Chopper

Widow finger chopper stone knife in plaited fiber. Believe it or not, widowed women from the Dani tribe in New Guinea chopped off the tip of one of their fingers as a physical sign of their grief and to keep bad spirits away.

ALL

WRAPPED

UP

HOLIDAY PRINCESS DRESS!

After tearing through gift-wrapped presents, most people throw away the leftover wrapping paper—but not Olivia Mears! The 26-year-old costume designer reuses the colorful material to create princess-style dresses, complete with bows and glitter!

Creating her first eco-conscious design in 2013, Mears posted photos of a red-and-gold paper dress to her social media pages, where she goes by avantgeek. The dresses are constructed using tape and glue instead of traditional needle and thread. Underneath each dress is a petticoat, which provides the wearer comfort and supports the weight of the wrapping paper. To make it easier to put on, the back of each dress laces up with the help of several coats of papier-mâché.

IN A HOLIDAZE

The largest gathering of people wearing holiday sweaters is 3,473, recorded at the University of Kansas on December 19, 2015.

Since 1974, it's a time-honored tradition to eat Kentucky Fried Chicken (KFC) on Christmas in Japan.

The largest display of lit Christmas trees was recorded on November 2, 2015, when the Hallmark Channel lit 559 Christmas trees in New York City's Herald Square.

If you keep your holiday lights up from Thanksgiving to New Years, and keep them on for 7 hours a day, your Christmas tree alone could cost you more than $15 a day!

U.S. shoppers reportedly spend $5 billion dollars on Christmas gifts for pets!

"Jingle Bells" was originally written for Thanksgiving, not Christmas!

PRECARIOUS PAGODA

Few landscapes prove as otherworldly as the Kyauk Ka Lat Pagoda near Mount Zwegabin in Hpa-An, Myanmar.

Balanced precariously on the limestone peak, the pagoda sits in an artificial lake where storks, egrets, and herons reign. While a tiny shrine about halfway up the rock face offers stunning views of the lake for adventurous souls, the actual summit remains, thankfully, off limits.

Fantastic Beasts

Hall Place in Bexley, England, features a topiary garden filled with the tamest monsters in the United Kingdom. Chris Riley, retired head gardener, spends one week each year trimming the hall's famous Queen's Beasts topiaries. This collection of 10 mythical creatures was planted in 1953 to commemorate the coronation of Queen Elizabeth II. The massive topiaries each represent a different heraldic beast associated with the monarch's genealogy, from the griffin to the dragon.

FLYING SOLO

Skirmantis Strimaitis was the only passenger on board a Boeing 737 flying from Vilnius, Lithuania, to Bergamo, Italy, on March 16, 2019. The airplane can seat up to 188 people, but the only others on board were the two pilots and five crew members.

WEIGHT LOSS

Cillas Givens, from Fairview, Oklahoma, lost 416 lb (189 kg)—more than the weight of two average men—in about two years. Before shedding more than half his body weight, he had weighed almost 730 lb (331 kg) and was so obese he could barely get out of bed for two and a half years.

BABY RACE

To mark International Children's Day, on June 1 each year, the Lithuanian capital of Vilnius stages a baby crawling race. As many as 25 babies crawl along a red carpet to the finish line, encouraged by family members waving toys and banging cans of baby food.

Weary Tides

The marine iguanas of the Galápagos Islands rely on the ocean as their sole food supply, but if their food source disappears, they sometimes simultaneously mummify and starve to death. Marine iguanas enjoy the simple pleasures in life: black lava for sunbathing and seaweed for grazing. But when El Niño weather patterns strike, these warm spells can cause the seaweed to die off. Without their primary food source, the iguanas waste away. Seated atop the black lava rock, they eventually succumb to starvation, leaving behind desiccated mummies.

Iguanas can shrink their bodies (and even their skeletons) as much as 20 percent to survive, but sometimes that's not enough.

KNIFE MADE FROM BONES!

BONE KNIFE

When a horrific motorcycle accident left Moreno Skvarca with a shattered leg, he teamed up with a friend to create a knife made out of his leg bone!

Doctors told Moreno that he would never walk again, but 10 months, seven surgeries, and a metal rod later, he defied the odds. To commemorate his ordeal, Moreno had a knife custom-made using two large bone fragments from his femur. Hand-forged by his friend, a bladesmith known as Emberborn, the knife blade includes an inscription in Slovenian that translates to "Life is not a piece of cake."

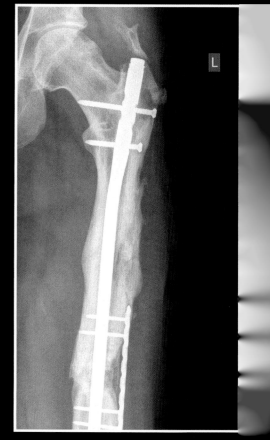

Moreno now has a metal rod in place of his femur bone, which was used to create the handle of the knife.

Donkey on a Hog

Sometimes farmers have to get a little creative when it comes to transporting livestock, especially in Koudougou, Burkina Faso, where bicycles and motorcycles are the primary forms of transportation. Remarkably, the donkey involved in this stunt looks surprisingly zen, despite being tied up and strapped to a makeshift basket. Something tells us this isn't the donkey's first ride.

PECULIAR PRESCRIPTIONS

In 1973, an obese 27-year-old Scottish man went on the most extreme diet imaginable when he fasted for 382 days under medical supervision, losing an extraordinary 276 lb (125 kg) with no ill effects.

Beer spas are all the buzz in Europe, Japan, and even parts of the American West Coast, because the yeast in bubbling brews is believed to boast cleansing properties and ease muscle and joint soreness.

For those suffering from sleep apnea, researchers in Switzerland have stumbled upon an effective, albeit impractical, new treatment option—playing the didgeridoo.

The treatment known as fecal bacteriotherapy involves a healthy person donating their poop so it can be liquified and transplanted into a sick person's butt, recolonizing their intestines with the healthy donor's bacterium in the process.

Some self-appointed health gurus tout the benefits of sungazing (staring directly into the sun), which has some eye doctors blind with rage, as it is actually very harmful to your eyes to stare at the sun and could even cause blindness.

Cryogenic chamber therapy is bringing new meaning to "icing down injuries" and involves entering a chamber (wearing no more than a bathing suit) for two to four minutes while liquid nitrogen drops the temperature to an average of –238°F (–150°C).

SWIMMING PRODIGY

Clark Kent Apuada, aged 10, swam the 100-meter butterfly in 1 minute 9.38 seconds at the Far Western Long Course Championship in his home state of California on July 29, 2018—more than a second faster than Michael Phelps did at the same age in 1995.

CHOPPED BRICKS

Chinese kung fu master Wang Hua used his bare hands to chop through 100 bricks in only 37 seconds.

TRAPEZE ARTIST

Betty Goedhart, of La Jolla, California, performs as a trapeze artist at age 86. She took up the daredevil circus discipline when she was 78 to overcome her fear of heights.

BACKFLIP SOMERSAULT

The Harlem Globetrotters' Will "Bull" Bullard landed a back somersault basketball shot from a distance of 58 ft 1 in (17.7 m) in Atlanta, Georgia, on October 21, 2018. Two months earlier, Bullard sank a basket with a ball thrown from an airplane as it flew over Woodbine, New Jersey.

HOCKEY TATTOOS

On April 6, 2019, seven-year-old Dyson Labossiere had his body decorated with 436 temporary tattoos of his favorite hockey team, the Winnipeg Jets.

CUFFED TOGETHER

Rebecca and Nuno Cesar de Sa, a married couple from West Yorkshire, England, ran the full 26.2 mi (42 km) of the 2019 London Marathon in 3 hours 43 minutes 17 seconds while handcuffed together.

HOLY GUACAMOLE

Chilean artist Boris Toledo makes portraits of iconic characters—including The Hulk, Homer Simpson, and Grumpy Cat—out of mashed avocado.

Toledo says he eats an avocado every day and was one day inspired to use the mushy green food to draw. His first avocado creation took 6 hours to make, but with practice he's down to one or two hours per drawing. After taking a photo of the portrait, he eats it.

VIVID VILLAGE

Every six months, people in one small Indonesian village paint their bodies in vivid colors and visit a temple to neutralize the ill effects of humanity on the environment.

Twice a year, the boys and men of Tegalalang Village in Bali cover their torsos and faces in bright paint and wear knickknacks and trinkets during the Ngerebeg Festival. Around 400 individuals from seven hamlets participate. Each hamlet is represented by a different hue—hence the villagers' color choices. The festival represents a restorative measure to counteract humanity's negative toll on the planet.

Misplaced Fireplace

On April 28, 2019, a man riding a bicycle was spotted in the UK town of Leigh balancing a fireplace around his neck. The English cyclist has brought new meaning to the old adage "Where there's a will, there's a way." After being spotted cruising down Westleigh Lane shouldering the massive hearth, photos of his dedication went viral, rendering him an overnight social media sensation.

SLEEP SYNDROME

Rhoda Rodriguez-Diaz, a student from Leicester, England, suffers from the rare "Sleeping Beauty" syndrome—a one-in-a-million condition that can cause her to sleep for 22 hours a day for up to three weeks at a time.

SURGERY JOKES

Comedian Sarah-May Philo, from Glasgow, Scotland, told jokes and sang songs while undergoing a nine-hour brain surgery. To test her brain function during the operation, she was kept fully conscious while surgeons removed a tumor.

IRISH ACCENT

After speech therapists and doctors had failed to find a solution, Nick Prosser, from Rotorua, New Zealand, cured his lifelong stutter by learning to speak in an Irish accent—even though he has never been to Ireland.

$100,000

The lottery jackpot that Christina LaBombard of Ashland, Virginia, won by using the numbers of her favorite NASCAR drivers.

HORSE FEAR

Notorious English-born highwayman Black Bart, who robbed at least 28 Wells Fargo stagecoaches in northern California between 1875 and 1883, was afraid of horses and carried out all of his robberies on foot.

CHARM BRACELET

As part of her sentence, U.S. District Judge Edward Lodge ordered Jennifer Fanopoulos, defendant in a court case in Boise, Idaho, to wear a charm bracelet bearing pictures of her children to discourage her from reoffending.

EARLY BABIES

Alya Juliette Mann, the first baby born in Saskatoon, Saskatchewan, Canada, in 2019, is the sister of Emery, the second baby born in Saskatoon in 2017. Both babies were born on January 1 to parents Graeme and Meagan Mann.

SPIDERS-MAN

Norwegian artist Dino Tomic recently created a Spider-Man portrait using countless tiny spider drawings.

Tomic used concepts found in pointillism to achieve the desired effect. When viewed at a distance, the portrait of actor Tom Holland looks stunningly lifelike, but step closer, and you'll see it relies on thousands of tiny spiders to create shadows and contrast. The intricate portrait only took a few days to complete, but it required plenty of patience and a passion for eight-legged creepy crawlies.

SHOT HIMSELF

A man in Detroit, Michigan, accidentally shot himself after throwing his shoe at a cockroach in an attempt to squash it. A gun hidden inside the sneaker went off and the bullet hit him in the foot.

NOISY BODY

Pam Roberts, from Kent, England, suffers from a rare condition where she can hear the sound of her own internal organs at work. Following a fall that created small holes in her left ear canal, she can constantly hear her blood pumping, her food digesting, her heart beating, and even her eyeballs moving from side to side.

A man who was house-sitting for his parents in Fresno, California, tried to use a blowtorch to kill some dangerous black widow spiders but instead succeeded in setting the home on fire.

HIDDEN TREASURE

Phoenix, Arizona, charity volunteer Cathy McAllister found $4,000 in a chamber cut inside a donated book, *The Decline and Fall of the Roman Empire*. She was about to throw out the book to be repurposed instead of sold, but before she did, she decided to leaf through the old classic. With the help of an accompanying family letter and address label, she was able to track down the owner and return the cash.

BED TESTERS

Mattress Firm, a national mattress chain based in Texas, employs "Snoozeterns" to spend up to 30 hours a week testing beds.

Bloody Fungi

Catching just one glimpse of the bleeding tooth fungus (*Hydnellum peckii*) is an experience you won't soon forget. This distinctive white mushroom oozes a thick scarlet fluid resembling blood. The underside of the cap has toothlike spines. Found in the Pacific Northwest and Europe, the fungus lives among moss and pine needle litter, where it quietly spends its time perfecting that horror movie vibe.

HEAVY METAL MAN

Rolf Buchholz of Germany holds the record for the most simultaneous piercings—480, to be exact.

Around his mouth and lips alone, he has 94. If that isn't enough, he recently added a pair of surgically implanted devil horns to his forehead. No word from airport security on how Buchholz fares going through metal detectors.

TOE BALL

A cross between cricket and golf, this Swiss sport uses a cow toe bone instead of a ball.

Switzerland is renowned for alpine scenery, the pastoral clink of cowbells, and the best-selling children's book *Heidi*. Although somewhat less romantic, the thwack of cow toe bones could also make the list. Why? Because the Swiss Alps boast the birthplace of Gilihuesine. To play, one athlete launches a bone off a log into the air with a bat while opposing players whack at it with massive wooden paddles. Winners take all (the beer, that is) when they knock the bone out of the air.

Some players will even throw their paddles in order to hit the soaring cow bone!

COW
TOE
BONES!

NINJA CAFÉ

Japan is well-known for eclectic themed cafés, but few like the Ninja Café and Bar, where you can dress, eat, drink, and fight like a ninja.

From its Shinto shrine–inspired entrance to its 39 tanuki statues, no detail has been spared when it comes to the Ninja Café and Bar in Tokyo's Asakusa District. Inside, visitors are greeted by walls lined with ninja weapons, including scythes, spears, and katanas. Food is served in the shape of shuriken (throwing stars). The café even offers lessons in katana wielding, dart blowing, shuriken throwing, and the ninja tea ceremony.

MAGGOT TREATMENT
After a bug bite on his toe while he was working in The Gambia, Africa, caused his foot to swell at an alarming rate, Matthew Blurton, from Doncaster, England, was diagnosed with a dangerous bacterial infection and flown back to the UK, where doctors used 400 specially bred maggots to eat away the dead flesh on his foot. The treatment was successful, but nurses were unable to remove all of the maggots and left 20 to decompose on his foot.

DRINKS BAN
In Britain during World War I, it was illegal to buy someone else a drink in a pub.

CHEWED HAIR
Doctors treating an eight-year-old girl, Feifei, for cramping pains in Guangdong, China, removed a 3-lb (1.4-kg) hairball from her stomach. She had been suffering from trichophagia, a condition where people feel compelled to eat their own hair, since she was two.

ROMAN HORSE
The 2,000-year-old remains of a horse still in its harness were uncovered in 2018 by archaeologists at a villa near Pompeii in Italy. Mount Vesuvius buried the ancient Roman city of Pompeii when it erupted in 79 AD.

LEMON HAUL
A man arrested in Riverside County, California, had 800 lb (363 kg) of stolen lemons in his car.

FAN FEED

WHOLE LOTTA LEMON!

LUDICROUS LEMON

Brent Ribnik of Florida wrote to Ripley's about his "giant lemon surprise"—or, more specifically, his 12-year-old Dwarf Meyer lemon tree that typically produces ping pong ball–sized fruit. About a year ago, he changed up the routine by giving it "special water," and something extraordinary happened. A lemon the size of a pink grapefruit appeared and has since gotten very ripe.

EVERY VOWEL

The only six-letter word in the English language that contains all five vowels is "eunoia," a rarely used medical term to describe a state of normal mental health.

PERFECT PITCH

On August 18, 2018, Sister Mary Jo Sobieck, a nun, threw the ceremonial first pitch in Chicago at the baseball game between the White Sox and the Kansas City Royals—and she delivered a perfect pitch.

FINE PRINT

Donelan Andrews, a high school teacher from Thomaston, Georgia, won $10,000 from a Florida travel insurance company because she took the trouble to read the fine print in a policy she had recently purchased. The secret contest was launched by St. Petersburg–based company Squaremouth, and buried in the fine print was a promise of $10,000 for the first person to send an e-mail to a specific address.

SAME SHOES

George W. Bush and Saddam Hussein had their expensive, thousand-dollar shoes handmade by the same Italian cobbler— Milan shoemaker Vito Artioli.

SHOPPER HIRE

To attract women to their stores, some shopping malls in China hire out handsome "shopping boyfriends" that women can rent by the hour to accompany them while they peruse for purchases.

BLOOD
VESSELS
INSIDE A
SHEEP'S
HEART

Ripley's Exhibit
Cat. No. 174052

Corrosion Cast
Sheep's Heart

Vascular corrosion
casting of a sheep's
heart. Resin was used to
capture the 3D structure
of blood vessels within
the tissue.

Ripley's Exhibit
Cat. No. 173727

Cigar Ash Portrait

Portrait of Taylor Swift made from cigar ashes. Created by Miguel Montero.

Ripley's Exhibit
Cat. No. 14922

Turtle Jewelry Box

Wooden jewelry box with tortoise shell veneer and carved ivory lattice work and feet. Picture of deer in the center.

inside the vault

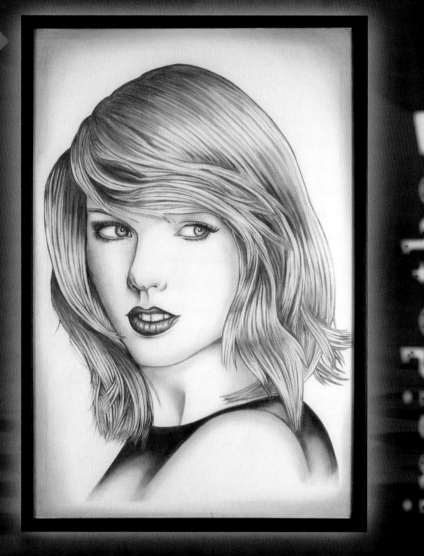

65 MILLION-YEAR-OLD SKELETON!

POPPY AND SAM ARE PROUD OF THEIR AMAZING FIND!

A FETCHING FIND

Two spunky pups named Poppy and Sam recently put a new twist on "fetching a bone." While strolling a beach in Somerset, England, with their owner, Jon Gopsill, they dug up a 65-million-year-old skeleton! Dating to the Jurassic period, scientists have identified it as an ichthyosaur—a toothy, porpoise-like sea creature that once ruled the deep.

A Claw Ahead

On November 2, 2019, spectators in Wuhan, China, gathered for a race that went a little sideways. Of course, they should have seen this coming since the competitors were crabs. Human observers used their hands to keep the crustaceans moving in the right direction, which led to some pinched results.

AIR
BUBBLE

SCUBA FLIES

The Mono Lake fly (*Ephydra hians*) envelopes its body in a protective air bubble to travel underwater without getting soaked.

Ever heard of six-legged scuba divers? If not, meet the Mono Lake fly, known for its unique ability to navigate the depths of what scientists call some of "the wettest water in the world." Three times saltier than your average lake, California's Mono has high pH, making it extra slippery and capable of drenching insects. Yet its namesake fly has found the ultimate way to explore the lake's subaqueous world while staying bone-dry.

COFFIN CUL

ETERNAL VOYAGE

For individuals searching for unique caskets, Crazy Coffins has the perfect answer.

They've spent 20 years designing custom final resting places with weird themes, from ballet slippers to luggage. As a result, they've garnered international acclaim and even a London Southbank exhibit. They've crafted sarcophagi inspired by Volkswagen Golfs and Mercedes vans. They've also brought to life pop-culture symbols, including the USS *Enterprise* for dearly departed Trekkies.

DYING TO DANCE!

RESERVED FOREVER!

CONSTRUCTION CASUALTIES

Russian gulag prisoners toiled on the White Sea–Baltic Canal from 1931 through 1933. At least 12,000 (but some estimate 25,000) perished due to dangerous and inhumane working conditions.

American workers labored furiously to complete the Hoover Dam (1931–1935), harnessing the power of the Colorado River. During construction, there were 96 recorded "industrial fatalities" due to falling rocks, drowning, and blasting.

It took two millennia for workers to construct the ambitious 13,000-mi-long (20,921-km) Great Wall of China. A rumored 400,000 laborers perished in the process, and many remain buried within the engineering marvel.

TURE RIP

REST
IN SPACE

DEPARTING
NOTES!

POLICE PUBLIC CALL BOX

POLICE TELEPHONE
FOR USE OF
PUBLIC
PHILIP
STILL BRINGING
US SUNSHINE
PULL TO OPEN

CALL
EXPIRED!

The Panama Canal (1880–1914) remains one of the most ambitious and deadly construction projects in modern history. Its final casualty count includes more than 25,000 workers, many of whom died of malaria and yellow fever.

Japanese forces compelled Burmese and Allied prisoners of war (POWs) to construct the Burma–Siam Railway (1942–1943) during World War II. An estimated 100,000 Burmese and more than 12,000 Allied POWs, along with tens of thousands of forced laborers, perished during its construction.

Among the deadliest construction projects in the United States, West Virginia's Hawks Nest Tunnel (1933–1935) led to more than 400 known direct deaths. Another 1,000 indirect casualties may have resulted from long-term exposure to silica dust, a by-product of the tunnel's construction.

ONE EYED PIGGIE

In Indonesia, a cyclops piglet, became a national sensation, with its physical deformities considered both a shock and a blessing to the farmer who owns him.

When Novli Rumondor decided to check on his sow's most recent family of 13 broods, he felt both stunned and amazed by what he found. One of the male piglets had facial deformities and one eye, symptoms consistent with a congenital condition known as *holoprosencephaly* or cyclops syndrome. Rumondor sees the piglet's birth as a blessing. People from across Indonesia have visited his farm to catch a glimpse of the remarkable piglet.

SLEEP TIGHT!

Buzz Buzzzzz

Busy bees need naps, too! Some species sleep in their hives, but others will curl up in a flower or lock their mandibles around a stem to keep themselves from falling as they doze off. When they reach a deep sleep, their antennae droop, their legs relax, and they become hard to wake up. If you come across a snoozing bee, observe from a distance and let them rest—they've earned it!

THIRSTY WORK
Elephants drink up to 50 gal (189 l) of water a day—enough to fill a standard bathtub or more than 900 glasses of water.

GOAT MAYOR
A three-year-old Nubian goat named Lincoln was elected mayor of Fair Haven, Vermont, in 2019, beating competition from dogs, cats, and a gerbil named Crystal.

FALLING HIVE
Strong winds in Phoenix, Arizona, caused a beehive to blow off a tree and land on the head of a woman who was walking below. She was stung more than 20 times around her head.

SUPER STINGER
Pulmonoscorpius kirktonensis—an extinct species of giant scorpion—was nearly 2.3 ft (0.7 m) long, making it bigger than a domestic cat.

SWALLOWED SKEWER
Hoshi, a six-year-old Shar-Pei dog owned by Sandra Kin of Glasgow, Scotland, had emergency surgery after swallowing an 8-in-long (20-cm) metal skewer along with a chicken kebab at a barbecue.

TEAR DRINKER
Gorgone macarea, a species of Brazilian moth, drinks the tears of sleeping birds. It sits on the neck of birds such as the black-chinned antbird and inserts its long proboscis into the bird's eye to suck up the liquid like a straw. The strange behavior is thought to be a way of obtaining salt, a vital nutrient that is not contained in flower nectar.

BEETLE JUICE
Nicrophorus vespilloides beetles lay their eggs on the buried carcasses of small birds or rodents, and to ensure that the corpse will remain fresh and bacteria-free for longer, the beetles use secretions from their anal glands to coat the fur or feathers with a form of disinfectant.

CLEVER DOG
Greg Basel's dog Marshall uses his nose to ring the doorbell of his house in Liberty Lake, Washington, so that he can be let in.

SHARK INVASION
A 330-lb (150-kg), 7-ft-long (2.1-m) bull shark suddenly jumped into the Chapman family's small boat while they were fishing on the Proserpine River in Queensland, Australia, on October 12, 2018. At the time, the Chapmans were concentrating on keeping a safe distance from a large crocodile they could see on the riverbank.

Seeing Double

Hazel, a beagle puppy in Yorkshire, UK, sent the internet into overdrive because of some strange markings on her coat that appear to reveal a self-portrait. On July 3, 2019, Shannon Austin did a double take after spotting a familiar image on her nine-week-old puppy's coat. She saw the distinct outline of a beagle on Hazel's back, with a different colored snout much like the puppy herself.

DOGGY DUPLICATE!

WORM BURGERS

Worm burgers are now for sale in the UK, and their creator, Horizon Edible Insects, claims they are "tastier than beef."

The company hopes their wormy burgers will promote more sustainable, environmentally friendly ways of eating. While this new meat alternative is not for the faint of heart, it comes with plenty of protein, vitamin B12, and omega-3s, while remaining low calorie. Delicious and nutritious!

TASTY!

DEER COLLISION
Christina Sanchez still finished the 2018 Jersey Shore Half Marathon at Sandy Hook, New Jersey, despite being taken out by a large deer partway around the course. A buck ran out of the woods and crashed into her, but after receiving medical attention, she was able to continue.

SOAP BUBBLES
In November 2018, Steven Langley, of Huntersville, North Carolina, put 13 people inside soap bubbles in 30 seconds. A performer with the Soap Bubble Circus, he has also created a hanging chain of 35 soap bubbles.

DAILY CLIMB
Rebecca Dooley, from Cumbria, England, hiked up a 1,400-ft-high (427-m) hill in the Lake District every day during 2018. Her 365 straight climbs meant she had scaled 17 times the height of Mount Everest.

SOCCER BOSS
Larry Barilli, an 83-year-old great-grandfather, has been a soccer manager for 66 years, taking charge of about 2,000 games. He started in 1953 and has coached amateur teams in and around Greenock, Scotland, ever since. He reckons that in all that time he has only ever missed seven games—through illness.

Card Collector

Former Tube engineer George Crupenschi has spent 15 years, and more than $12,922 (£10,000), collecting empty Oyster cards. The white-and-blue cards are used to pay for transportation around London and appear very similar to the untrained eye. But Crupenschi has made distinguishing the subtle differences of his 1,000+ card collection a point of personal expertise.

UNFORGETTABLE DAY
Ali Gibb, a 51-year-old amateur golfer, made three holes-in-one on a single day. Playing in a 36-hole competition at Croham Hurst Golf Club in Surrey, England, on August 14, 2018, she aced the fifth hole in both rounds and also recorded a hole-in-one at the 11th on her second round.

ROCK CLIMBER
Despite being born without a lower left arm, Maureen Beck, from Arvada, Colorado, is a skilled rock climber, and in 2018 she scaled the Lotus Flower Tower, an 8,470-ft-high (2,582-m) granite peak in Canada's Northwest Territories.

WATER TANK
Vako Marchelashvili solved six Rubik's Cubes underwater in a single breath in Tbilisi, Georgia. He was submerged in a glass tank for 1 minute 44 sec, having trained for the challenge for six months.

TRAIL HIKER
Heather "Anish" Anderson, from Michigan, walked 7,944 mi (12,710 km) through 22 U.S. states in 251 days in 2018, averaging 31 mi (50 km) a day and wearing through a pair of shoes every 20 days. Since 2013, she has speed-hiked 28,000 trail miles (45,000 km)—further than walking the entire length of the Equator.

THERAPEUTIC HORNS

Take a walk down the streets of Jakarta, and you might see strange-looking individuals sitting cross-legged with what appear to be multiple horns growing out of their backs.

They're partaking in a thousands-of-years-old cupping therapy to improve circulation and dampen pain. Instead of heated glass cups, Indonesian street healers use buffalo horns to stimulate the flow of energy inside the body.

HOOKED

A group of thrill seekers glided above Thailand while suspended from parachutes attached to their backs with massive hooks!

Parasailing typically involves being pulled through the sky behind a boat while wearing a harness connected to a small parachute, but these suspension enthusiasts cut out the middle man and attached the parachute directly to their skin. They pierced small metal rods through their backs, secured hooks onto the rods, and then clipped the parachute onto the hooks. Amazingly, they were able to soar above the water just like a standard parasailer.

Avo-Control!

Self-described Australian eco-warrior Marissa Hush has decided to fight climate change by cultivating avocado trees using seeds rescued from cafés and restaurants. Hush pots the seeds in plastic cups found on beaches and in the street. She stumbled across this mission after moving to Vietnam. It began with saving each avocado stone that she ate but eventually evolved into a goal to grow 500 avocado trees. Despite the fact it takes an avocado tree up to 15 years to mature, Hush remains dedicated and plans on eventually planting each one in the wild.

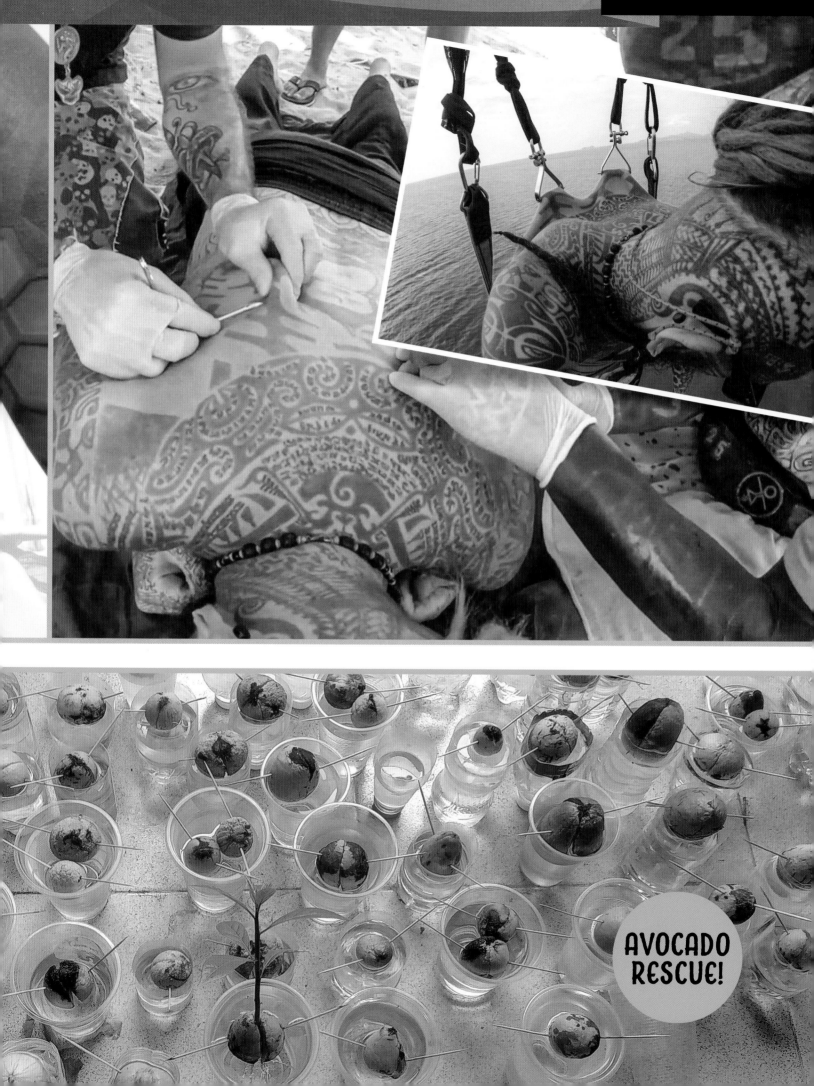

AVOCADO RESCUE!

RIPLEY'S EXCLUSIVE

AMPUTEE
ATHLETES

No matter their age or location, amputees are often told they may be unable to continue doing what they love. Dedication, perseverance, and a thirst for the thrill are what drive any athlete to compete. For these amputee athletes, congenital or not, they don't let fear get in the way of their passion to be the best in their field.

MAKING A SPLASH!

FOUR-TIME PARALYMPIC CHAMPION!

Rudy Garcia-Tolson, 31, of Bloomington, California, was born with a rare birth defect, popliteal pterygium syndrome.

Wheelchair-bound at the age of five, having already undergone 15 surgeries, Garcia-Tolson had both legs amputated above the knees. What may sound like a challenging decision actually provided Garcia-Tolson with greater mobility and the opportunity to live a full, active life with the aid of prosthetics.

Garcia-Tolson began swimming, and then running, at just six years old. He is a four-time Paralympic swimmer and has participated in the Ironman Triathlon.

Q: HOW DID YOU GET INVOLVED WITH SPORTS?

A: I was always a fan of the water, even though I was terrified of drowning and didn't know how to swim. My dad suggested I take swim lessons three times a week for a few months to learn the basics and learn to swim without legs. My instructor suggested I join a club or swim team and try to do some races.

Q: HOW DID YOU TRAIN AND PREPARE FOR AN EVENT?

A: In middle school, I would swim for two-hour sessions six times a week in the pool. In high school, it was seven or eight times a week. During the Olympics, it was nine times a week with additional gym time three days a week. At the Olympics, I was swimming anywhere from 50–60 thousand meters (31–38 miles) a week! Sometimes I would get a massage or do yoga to relieve the stress on my body.

Q: WHAT'S YOUR BIGGEST MOTIVATION?

A: When I was younger, my goal was just to swim faster than a kid with legs. I became involved with the Challenged Athletes Foundation, and they really motivated me to build my confidence. As an adult, it's cool to mentor other kids through the Challenged Athletes Foundation and be someone they can look up to for guidance.

Q: WHAT WAS YOUR GUILTY PLEASURE SNACK WHILE TRAINING?

A: I have a special relationship with Flamin' Hot Cheetos! I also enjoyed eating a lot of pizza. I was not the model athlete when it came to my diet.

Q: WHAT'S BEEN AN UNEXPECTED CHALLENGE?

A: As a kid growing up with a disability, I struggled to be comfortable with who I was. I used to wear pants all the time, I didn't want to be on TV, and I was embarrassed when my friends saw me. Nowadays, living in New York City is the only challenge I face. With the crowds and all the stairs that sometimes don't have handrails, it can be difficult to navigate the city. But I've gotten comfortable with adapting to my environment.

Q: WHAT IS YOUR FONDEST MEMORY OF YOUR CAREER?

A: There's nothing like my first Paralympic experience. It was my dream that I envisioned as a kid, and it came true. I wanted to be on the winners' blocks, and I kept that goal in mind. At my first event, I shaved about 10 seconds off my time. I was in disbelief. I won my first gold medal. I slept with it under my pillow the whole next week!

Q: WHAT ARE YOU DOING NOW?

A: I work with a running organization called the New York Road Runners. I'm part of the Youth Wheelchair Program, which is for physically challenged kids, and we supply all the sports equipment needed to have practices every week. I am a firm believer that sports are a vehicle for kids with disabilities to build their confidence and show them they can accomplish anything, regardless of their level of ability.

Half-Pipe Hero

Vinicios Sardi, 23, of São Paulo, Brazil, has perfected the art of skateboarding without legs, and the gravity-defying tricks that he performs are out of this world! Born with a congenital malformation of both legs and his right hand, Sardi learned how to skateboard on prosthetics. But he quickly realized they couldn't hold up to the wear and tear of extreme sports. Skating on his knees, Sardi's talent and love for the sport quickly soared, making him a force of nature at the skate park.

SKATEBOARDING SENSATION!

Tackling the Odds

Chris Young, 27, of the United Kingdom, was born with a congenital amputation just below his right elbow, but that hasn't stopped him from playing competitive rugby and even leading the team! As captain of the North Yorkshire rugby union team Selby Fours, he's steered his squad to third in their league.

ONE-ARMED RUGBY CHAMPION!

1 PIECE, 2 IMAGES!

Ripley's Exhibit
Cat. No. 174015

The Wolves Come Out at Night

Aluminum foil shaped into a crescent moon. The peaks and valleys create either a shadow or an outline of a howling wolf, depending on the angle of the light source. Created by Pam Hage, winner of Ripley's Unconventional Art Contest with DeviantArt in 2018.

Ripley's Exhibit
Cat. No. 173912

Woolly Rhinoceros Skull

Skull of the prehistoric Siberian woolly rhinoceros, *Coelodonta antiquitatis*. The species went extinct around 8000 BC.

inside the vault

xhibit

73956

arousel

moving carousel with taxidermy
and a lizard, instead of horses.
bugs include a walking stick,
eetle, sunset moth, and a tarantula.
Brian and Stephanie Magby

KEEP ON TRUCKIN'

This Italian motor show took vehicle stunt tricks to the next level with a semitruck demo that appeared to rewrite the laws of physics.

Driving stunts such as popping wheelies and skiing (where a car balances on two wheels) have become increasingly popular at car shows. Movies such as *The Fast and the Furious* (and its many sequels) have made such tricks downright commonplace. But seeing semitrucks perform the same feats? Utterly mind-blowing. Just ask the lucky fans in attendance at the 2010 Bologna Motor Show in Italy.

CARTOON CAFÉ

Café Yeonnam-dong 239-20 in Seoul, South Korea, is designed to make customers feel as if they are appearing in an animated fantasy series.

The cartoon decor was inspired by the popular South Korean fantasy TV show *W: Two Worlds*, about a cartoonist's daughter who gets pulled into her dad's animated world. The café has proven popular, partially because of the fun pictures people are able to capture in the unique setting.

MAKING FOOD

Set your plate down and take another look—these mouth-watering dishes are actually handmade embroidery! Using a needle and thread as her paintbrush, Japanese embroidery artist Ipnot creates miniature masterpieces one French knot at a time. Combining and choosing from 500 different colors of yarn, Ipnot spends anywhere between three to ten hours on each delicate "plate."

For his series "People," Italian artist Stefano Bolcato recreated famous paintings by the likes of Botticelli, Leonardo da Vinci, and Andy Warhol by painting the subjects as LEGO minifigures.

TOBACCO PORTRAIT
Egyptian artist Abdelrahman al-Habrouk creates portraits of famous people, such as Johnny Depp, out of burnt tobacco. He arranges the flakes of tobacco into an image on white paper, then sprinkles it with gunpowder and sets it on fire. The resulting scorch marks left on the paper form the portrait.

MYSTERY CODE
Between 1881 and 1887, English children's author Beatrix Potter kept a journal in which she wrote her private thoughts in a secret code that was so complex it was not cracked until 1958.

TV WRITER
Suzanne Collins, author of *The Hunger Games* trilogy of novels, was one of the writers on the 1990s children's TV show *Clarissa Explains It All*.

COFFEE MONSTERS
German designer Stefan Kuhnigk turns random coffee stains into cartoon monsters. He created his first Coffee Monster after seeing the stain that his cup of dark espresso left on a piece of paper. He now uses a spoon to spill coffee on sheets of paper every day and has so far completed more than 600 pictures.

BARBIE SHRINE
Japanese-born Azusa Sakamoto has turned her Los Angeles home into a shrine to Barbie. She has spent more than $70,000 converting her home into a giant Barbie house, with every detail—right down to drinking glasses—either pink or Barbie-themed. Sakamoto has also dyed her hair pink and only wears clothes that are pink or feature the Barbie logo.

ELVIS SONGS
Lilo & Stitch, a 2002 Disney film, features more Elvis Presley songs than any of Presley's own films.

GOING BANANAS!

Bananas take on new life as intricate carvings under the knife—or toothpick—of Japanese artist Keisuke Yamada.

Banana carving may not be your idea of a fun Saturday night, but for Yamada, an electrician by day, the elongated fruit is the perfect canvas for his sculptures of animals and pop culture figures. Yamada started carving the fruit in 2011 to alleviate boredom. Today, he's created countless masterpieces and internet sensations. The unassuming artist attributes the realistic nature of his work to the texture of the bananas, but it's hard to deny the talent of this Michelangelo of tropical fruit.

THAT'S BANANAS!

On a state-by-state basis, Walmart's best-selling items include everything from antifreeze to dog treats. But as a nation, the number one best-selling item in the United States is bananas.

Banana trees aren't trees at all but rather the world's largest herb. Strangely, bananas are technically berries—an honor that raspberries and strawberries don't even enjoy.

Humans and bananas share a genetic similarity of 60 percent! A printed version of your genetic code would occupy 262,000 pages, but only 500 of those are unique to humans.

There are more than 1,000 different types of bananas in existence! The Cavendish is the most common and most widely exported type worldwide.

What's yellow and black and weighs 28 lb (13 kg)? The supply of bananas the average American consumes each year.

Bananas grow in clusters called "hands," and individual fruits are known as "fingers." Many hands of bananas make up a larger stalk referred to as a "bunch," which contains as many as 170 bananas.

FIRST WRITING

While North Americans celebrate education with "Back to School" sales and kindergarten graduations, first graders in China attend a "wisdom eye-opening" ceremony.

Dressed in traditional Chinese clothing, groups of children near Hancheng Lake in Xi'an participate in the ancient "first writing ceremony." During the event, a red dot is painted on each student's forehead, a symbol of "the opening of the wisdom eye." With this ceremony, children are introduced into the lifelong pursuit of learning.

Garland King

Every May 29th, a quaint village in Derbyshire Peak District, England, celebrates Garland Day with a flower-obscured king on horseback. The Garland Ceremony in the village of Castleton remains a bizarre event with mysterious origins. It requires the star of the parade, the "Garland King," to wear a heavy, bell-shaped frame covered completely in flowers and greenery. While some believe the event commemorates the restoration of Charles II in 1660, after he was forced to hide out in an oak tree, not everyone agrees. Others argue it's a representation of the much older Jack in the Green. Today, the procession's origins remain as hidden as the "Garland King" himself.

WHAT'S THE WORD

RUN

"Run" is one of the most complex words in the English language. The verb form alone has 645 different meanings listed in the Oxford English Dictionary.

COLOR

In every language, blue was the last color to get a word. Black and white, or light and dark, are the first to appear, and red is always next, usually followed by yellow. It's theorized that blue is last because it rarely appears in nature and knowledge of the color isn't necessary for survival.

◀DIRECTION▶

Kuuk Thaayorre, a language spoken by an Aboriginal community in northern Australia, has no words for relative directions like "left," "right," "ahead," or "behind." Instead, the speakers use cardinal directions like north, south, east, and west to orient themselves and everything around them.

Wing Transplant

Believe it or not, by using a wing from a deceased butterfly, a glass plate, some superglue, and very delicate movements, Katie VanBlaricum of Kansas was able to replace an injured monarch butterfly's wing, facilitating its release back into the wild.

After surgery

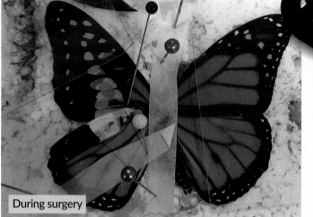
During surgery

SPEED JUMPER
Daifuku, a Jack Russell terrier, jumped over Japanese owner Hiroaki Uchida's leg 37 times in 30 seconds at a talent show in Hong Kong.

FUR CHANGE
Elli, a cat from Germany, has vitiligo, a rare condition that has caused her fur to go from black to almost completely white in just one year.

FAKE SNAKE
If attacked, the Eurasian wryneck—a small brown woodpecker—imitates a snake by bending and twisting its head from side to side and hissing menacingly.

LONG LIFE
George, a goldfish won at a fair in 1974 by Keith Allies from Worcester, England, lived to the age of 44. The average life expectancy of a goldfish is 10 years!

SLOW HEARTBEAT
A blue whale's heart beats as low as two times a minute when diving, which is 30 to 50 percent lower than scientists thought.

COOL BEAR
A bear climbed into Mark Hough's backyard in Altadena, California, enjoyed a dip in his jacuzzi for a few minutes, and drank a leftover margarita before falling asleep in a nearby tree.

FAN FEED

Painting Parrot

Gina Keller of Ontario, Canada, reached out to Ripley's to share her painting parrot! Keller adopted three-year-old Koa, a male sun conure, and has since taught him dozens of tricks, including painting on a small canvas that sits on a tiny art easel using miniature, 2-in (0.39-cm) paintbrushes, which he holds in his beak. Some of the proceeds from the sale of Koa's paintings goes to charity. Koa entertains and amazes fans all over the world on Instagram: @koa_tiko.

FEAR WORM

Believe it or not, this isn't a worm or a snake. It's a legless amphibian called a caecilian, and its smooth and slimy outer appearance hide a mouthful of needle-sharp teeth. Some species even let their babies eat their mother's flesh!

CRAZY ROWS OF TEETH!

There are more than 200 species of caecilians, with some growing only 3.5 in (8.9 cm) and others growing as big as a human at nearly 5 ft (1.5 m). They come in all kinds of colors—orange, black, purple, yellow, green, and blue—and they may or may not need their eyes, since they tend to live in the soil. But since the carnivores also eat a variety of animals (like lizards, snakes, frogs, termites, beetles, and even other caecilians), the beasts wield an impressive array of chompers, all the better to grab their prey and swallow it whole (like a snake).

The *Boulengerula taitana* species of Kenya takes the trophy for the best mother, however. This mama grows a thicker layer of skin for her babies to peel off and eat. The behavior is called *dermatotrophy* and it's only exhibited in caecilians.

CLAIM TO FLAME

One of the most dramatic tribal displays in the world, the Baining Fire Dance of Kokopo, Papua New Guinea, requires masked dancers to run through flames.

The dance takes place on the island of New Britain. Performers wear abstract masks and ones that may represent various animals. These masks are said to help them communicate with the spirit realm. After entering a trance-like state, dancers take turns running through the flames, kicking up glowing clouds of embers along the way.

REVERSE FLOW
Violent storms and strong winds routinely cause waterfalls in Cumbria, England, to reverse and flow upward.

LOBSTER POT TREES
Communities in New England and along Canada's east coast build huge Christmas trees using carefully stacked lobster pots. The finished towers are then decorated with colorful buoys instead of Christmas lights.

BLACK SNOW
The Russian cities of Kiselyovsk and Prokopyevsk experienced toxic black snow in February 2019. The heavy snow that had fallen turned black overnight due to severe pollution in the coal mining region.

PANCAKE PAPER
The only scientific paper ever published by Bill Gates was a possible solution in the early 1970s to a mathematical problem about flipping pancakes.

WELSH OUTPOST
More than 7,000 mi (11,200 km) from Wales, there is a Welsh-speaking settlement of Patagonia, Argentina, called Y Wladfa, where people speak in their own distinctive Welsh dialect.

KICKBOXING GRANNIES
Grandmothers in their seventies living in Korogocho, a tough district of Nairobi, Kenya, have taken up kickboxing to defend themselves.

Putt Putt Parish

Rochester Cathedral, located outside of London, recently infused new meaning into the word "multipurpose" by installing a miniature golf course. The course was slated to open for only about a month. But that didn't dampen the ire of some locals who called it an "act of desecration." What motivated the unlikely golf course installation? The hopes of drawing more individuals to the cathedral who might not otherwise visit. To avoid alienating church regulars, the course was not open during scheduled services.

DON'T TRY THIS AT HOME!

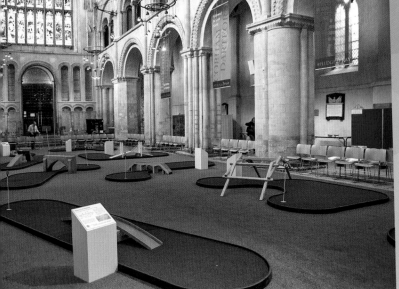

![Ripley's Believe It or Not!]

Ripley's Exhibit

Cat. No. 5557

Feather Coil Money

Feather coil money from the Santa Cruz Islands. This bird feather money was made from the head feathers of the cardinal myzomela and was used in virtually all financial transactions. Ripley collected this sample in 1932, which was made by overlapping 50,000 red feathers from hundreds of birds.

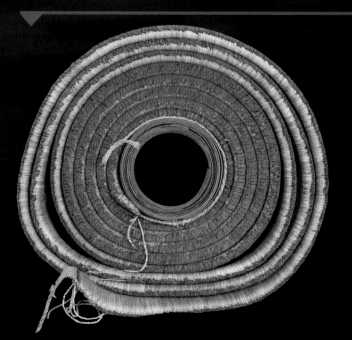

Ripley's Exhibit

Cat. No. 5731

Tea Brick Money

Chinese tea brick money. In Mongolia, Tibet, and many other provinces in China, tea was compressed into bricks and given as wages.

Ripley's Exhibit
Cat. No. 168260

$100 Bill Nail Art

A $100 bill recreated on a 7 x 3 ft (2.1 x 0.9 m) piece of wood with more than 20,000 nails. Hammered one nail at a time by artist Gary A. Winter of Pleasanton, California.

Ripley's Exhibit
Cat. No. 166176

Pillow Money Box

Large lacquer money box and pillow. A person in China would store his or her valuables in this box and use it as a pillow to prevent theft as they slept.

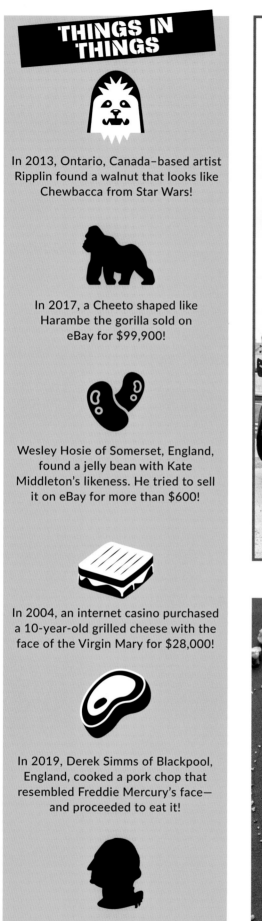

THINGS IN THINGS

In 2013, Ontario, Canada–based artist Ripplin found a walnut that looks like Chewbacca from Star Wars!

In 2017, a Cheeto shaped like Harambe the gorilla sold on eBay for $99,900!

Wesley Hosie of Somerset, England, found a jelly bean with Kate Middleton's likeness. He tried to sell it on eBay for more than $600!

In 2004, an internet casino purchased a 10-year-old grilled cheese with the face of the Virgin Mary for $28,000!

In 2019, Derek Simms of Blackpool, England, cooked a pork chop that resembled Freddie Mercury's face—and proceeded to eat it!

Rebekah Speight of Dakota City, Nebraska, sold a three-year-old chicken nugget resembling George Washington's face for $8,100!

Grass Guzzler

This car takes eco-friendly vehicles to the next level! Created in Japan by Nobuya Ushio, a landscaping business owner, this Nissan 350 Z was his ultimate marketing tool. With artificial turf being one of his most popular items, Ushio spent over a month building his rolling advertisement.

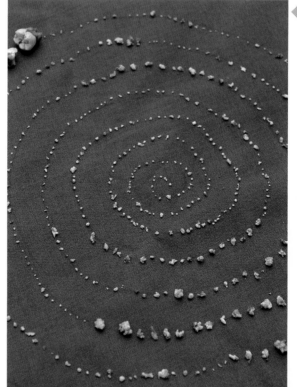

Too Many Teeth

A seven-year-old boy in India recently underwent surgery to have 526 teeth removed from his lower right jaw. Before the discovery, the boy complained of a toothache and visible swelling near his lower right molars. An X-ray revealed a strange sac embedded in his jaw—a rare condition known as compound composite odontoma. Two surgeons and a team of medical personnel removed the sac and confirmed its contents: a total of 526 teeth ranging in size from 0.004 to 0.6 in (0.1 to 1.5 cm). While incredibly small, each tooth had a root, crown, and enamel coat.

DJ HOOKIE

Despite losing both arms and legs to a bloodstream infection at age 19, this groundbreaking DJ has inspired countless fans.

Tom Nash, aka DJ Hookie, has never let the fear of failure or the loss of his four limbs get in the way of success. The talented 36-year-old from Sydney, Australia, has not only risen to prominence in the electronic music world, but he's also a top-notch motivational speaker that people travel from all over the world to see. What's the secret behind his success? According to Nash, the hooks that he uses (instead of prosthetic arms) allow him to spin music like nobody else.

LUCKY PENNY
A dented 1889 penny that saved the life of British Army Private John Trickett when it deflected an enemy bullet during World War I sold at auction in 2019 for $5,000. He would have been shot in the heart, but instead the coin he kept in his breast pocket sent the bullet ricocheting up his nose and out through the back of his left ear, leaving him deaf in that ear but alive.

DOUBLE TROUBLE
Twins Dave and Paul Dooley, both retired military driving tutors, were fined for speeding on the same road, on the same morning, at exactly the same speed. Both were doing 35 mph (56 kmph) rather than the legal limit of 30 mph (48 kmph) on Winwick Road, Warrington, England, on July 1, 2014. This is the second time the twins have been clocked for speeding on the same day.

44 CHILDREN
Mariam Nabatanzi Babirye, from Uganda's Mukono District, gave birth to 44 children by age 40—eight singles, six sets of twins, four sets of triplets, and three sets of quadruplets.

PRESERVED PIES
A perfectly preserved tin of mince pies from World War II was put on display in a museum in 2018 after being discovered beneath the floorboards of the Loch Hotel in Douglas, Isle of Man, off the northwest coast of England. The air-tight conditions under the hotel floor had helped keep the treats fresh for more than 70 years.

FULL HOUSE
From 1995 to 2001, every seat at Jacobs Field, now Progressive Field (home of the Cleveland Indians baseball team), was sold out—a run of 455 games straight.

SHIPWRECKED SAILOR
In 1784, Chunosuke Matsuyama, a shipwrecked Japanese sailor, carved a message into thin pieces of wood from a coconut tree, put it in a bottle, and tossed it into the ocean in the hope that someone might find him on the Pacific island where he and his crew were stranded. The bottle eventually washed ashore 151 years later in 1935 in Hiraturemura, the village where Matsuyama was born.

TWO WOMBS
Proud mother Arifa Sultana has two functioning wombs and in 2019 gave birth to twins at a hospital in Dhaka, Bangladesh, just 26 days after giving birth to a single baby boy. The rare condition, called uterus didelphys, affects about one in a million women. Doctors only discovered she had the condition when she surprisingly gave birth for the second time.

DUEL OF THE FATES

The land of *The Three Musketeers*, France long ago perfected the art of swordplay and is back at it again with the newly minted sport of lightsaber fighting.

Do you ever find yourself fantasizing about acting out your favorite lightsaber scene from *Star Wars*? If so, buy a plane ticket to France, where lightsaber dueling just got added to the official rulebook of the French Fencing Federation. The federation has even started equipping local fencing clubs with lightsabers and created a training program for instructors, all in the hopes of getting sedentary kids off the couch and onto the fencing strip.

COMPETITORS AT THE 2016 ARTISTIC FENCING WORLD CHAMPIONSHIP!

TV MARATHON
Having never previously viewed a single episode, Andrei Akimov spent a week locked in a glass cube in a theater in Moscow, Russia, watching the entire first seven seasons of *Game of Thrones*. He watched the TV for 10 hours every day and was only allowed to leave the cube to go to the toilet.

WARCRAFT LESSON
In 2005, a glitch in *World of Warcraft* allowed a plague to spread in the video game, resulting in non-infected players abandoning their cities while infected players were forced into quarantine. The fantasy situation was later studied by scientists to determine how people would react to a real-life pandemic.

UNKNOWN ARTIST
A 1964 art exhibition in Gothenburg, Sweden, featured paintings by an unknown French abstract artist called Pierre Brassau. The critics were impressed, with one saying, "Pierre is an artist who performs with the delicacy of a ballet dancer." It was later revealed that Pierre was a chimpanzee from the local zoo.

FANFEED

1,300 BALLOONS

MASSIVE MINION

Brothers Richard and Preston Roy of Weyburn, Saskatchewan, Canada, shared with us this 13-ft-tall (4-m) Minion costume that they crafted out of 1,300 balloons! The brothers wove various sizes of latex balloons together in intricate cross patterns to create the finished product. It took nearly 50 hours to build and required two people to maneuver! The creation was featured in a local parade highlighting the city's creativity.

SHORT FLIGHT

Frank Sinatra used to take his private jet from Los Angeles to Palm Springs—less than 30 minutes of flying time.

NO WEAPONS

The iTunes user agreement requires that you do not use iTunes to develop, design, or manufacture nuclear weapons.

CHOCOLATE TASTER

As a schoolboy in Derbyshire, England, Roald Dahl, author of *Charlie and the Chocolate Factory*, was an enthusiastic taste tester for Cadbury's chocolate. Each year, he and his schoolmates at Repton School would be sent a number of prospective new Cadbury products to try out.

SPIRITS' SEATS

Two seats at the Palace Theatre in London, England, are permanently left down for the theatre ghosts to sit in.

TOO YOUNG

Dick Van Dyke needed old-age makeup for his role in *Mary Poppins Returns* because he looked younger than his 93 years.

Hoverbike

For the motorcyclist who has everything, here's the perfect gift: the Lazareth LMV 496 La Moto Volante. This veritable "flying motorcycle" looks like something straight out of a sci-fi movie. And when its wheels move from their upright to horizontal positions for flight, the bike could be Optimus Prime's baby brother.

ROLLING ON

Ross Pollock, from Portsmouth, England, traveled 874 mi (1,398 km)—equivalent to the length of Britain—on roller skates. It took him 86 days, and he wore through four sets of wheels and lost 56 lb (25 kg) in weight.

DISNEY PARKS

On October 17, 2018, Heather and Clark Ensminger, from Kingsport, Tennessee, visited every Disney Park in the United States in 20 hours. After visiting the four parks on the East Coast in the Orlando, Florida, area, they flew 2,500 mi (4,000 km) over two time zones to visit the remaining two parks on the West Coast near Anaheim, California.

TIGHT FIT

On February 17, 2019, father-of-two Ted Hastings wore 260 T-shirts simultaneously in Kitchener, Ontario, Canada, in sizes up to 20XL. He managed to put the first 20 shirts on unaided but needed help with the rest.

MOWER MARATHON

Andy Maxfield, from Lancashire, England, rode a regular sit-on lawnmower the entire length of Britain from John O'Groats, Scotland, to Land's End, Cornwall. He covered the 874 mi (1,398 km) in 5 days 8 hours and 36 minutes, reaching a top speed of almost 10 mph (16 kmph).

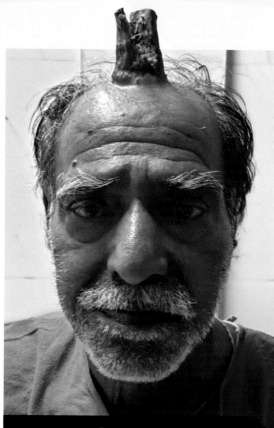

Horned Man

Shyam Lal Yadav has a new lease on life thanks to surgery in Sagar City, India, to remove a 4-in (10.16-cm) horn from the crown of his head. According to surgeon Dr. Vishal Gajbhiye, the thick spike started growing about five years ago following an injury to Yadav's head. A sebaceous horn, it's made of keratin, the same material as toenails and human hair.

MODEL CONTRACT

In 2019, New York City–born Iris Apfel landed a major modeling contract at age 97—with the same agency that represents Gigi Hadid, Karlie Kloss, and Miranda Kerr.

JENGA STACK

In January 2019, Tai Star Valianti, from Pima, Arizona, stacked 353 Jenga blocks atop a single upright block.

MINIATURE BODYBUILDER

Rakhim Kurayev, a six-year-old boy from Chechnya, Russia, performed 4,618 consecutive push-ups, taking just over two hours. His amazing display of strength previously won him a real $30,000 Mercedes car and a trip to a toy shop where he could buy everything he wanted.

SOCCER VETERAN

Colin Lee, from Northampton, England, still plays as goalkeeper for a local amateur soccer team at age 80. His soccer career started when he was six, and he has kept goal since 1949, despite now having arthritis in his hands and knees.

METAL MAULER

Using only his bare hands, professional strongman Bill Clark tore 23 U.S. government-issued metal license plates in half in one minute in Binghamton, New York.

After one show in Montreal, a little boy asked if Mama Lou could break pencils with her butt. "I looked at him with all my strongwoman-ness and I said, 'Probably. Yeah.' I went home that night to my room, got an entire box of pencils, and shut the door. And I didn't come out until I could bust those things with my butt muscles."

STRONG WOMAN

Linsey Lindberg of Kansas City, Kansas, moved to New York City, joined a clown troupe, and then trained as an aerialist before realizing her body was incredibly tough and strong (rather than flexible). Thus, Mama Lou, the American Strong Woman, was born.

Mama Lou can tear phone books in half, crush apples with her biceps, roll metal frying pans into tubes, pound nails into wood with her bare hands, and even snap pencils with her butt. Her favorite trick to perform is one she invented— potato-sack lifting with her tongue! She says she can lift 10 lb (4.5 kg) of potatoes using just her tongue, arguably the most versatile muscle in the human body.

Unbelievably, Mama Lou doesn't train with weights or machines herself, but instead simply practices what she wants to do. "The best way to smash an apple with your bicep," she says, "is to put an apple in there and do it."

HIDDEN MEMO

Are you an armchair archaeologist who secretly longs to discover lost cities buried in overgrown jungles and desert dunes? Then this pad's for you! The square cube of paper note cards appears unassuming, but as you tear away its pages, a tiny laser-cut city emerges. To excavate the entire sculpture, you'll have to exhaust the memo pad, revealing an intricate, hidden world.

FINISHED!

SMART PARK

When Hurricane Dorian threatened to make landfall in Florida in September 2019, a Jacksonville resident took extreme measures to keep his smart car from blowing away; he parked it in the kitchen! Patrick Eldridge chose the kitchen because his wife's vehicle already filled the garage.

SPEAR SURVIVOR

Despite impaling his face with a spear gun, Reverend Connie Hallowell lived to tell the tale!

While spearfishing in the sea off Scottburgh Beach south of Durban, the South African priest accidentally launched the 3-ft (0.9-m) dart into his face while attempting to remove sinkers from rocks. The projectile smashed through his right cheek, exiting in front of his left ear. Remarkably, the spear missed his brain and eyes. Despite the grisly injury, he walked ashore, where lifeguards treated him. A local fisherman used an angle grinder to shorten the spear's length so that Connie could be airlifted to the hospital. There, doctors removed the spear.

Deadly Dentures

A practicing and licensed dentist in Tampa, Florida, Michael Foley has collected shark teeth since he was six years old. Now at 33, he decided to combine his two passions. He created a pair of dentures using two rows of razor sharp fossil shark teeth. This set of both upper and lower teeth makes for a pretty sinister set of chompers!

SINGING SAMOYED

Ghost, a Samoyed dog owned by Norwegians Aline Tøllefsen Søndrol and Kristoffer Rosenberg, "sings" along so well to artists such as Beyoncé, Gwen Stefani, and Imagine Dragons that she has more than 370,000 fans on her Instagram page and even has her own manager in the United States.

EXPLODING MOOSE

Wildlife managers in Bridger-Teton National Forest, Wyoming, used 100 lb (45.4 kg) of explosives to blow up the carcass of a dead moose to stop it from attracting scavenging wolves and mountain lions in a popular hiking area.

ZEBRA STRIPES

It is possible that one of the reasons zebras have stripes is to deter bloodsucking flies. Scientists dressed horses in black and white striped coats and found that fewer horseflies landed on them than on horses that were not wearing the coats.

STARVATION MODE

Nearly microscopic tardigrades—or water bears—can go without food for a decade and can survive in environments as diverse as hot springs, Antarctic glaciers, and the bottom of the ocean.

GOLF BALLS

Veterinary surgeons removed five golf balls from the stomach of Louis, a springer spaniel Labrador mix. He had swallowed them over the course of a few months while walking on a golf course near his home in Birmingham, England, with his owner Rebecca Miles.

SINISTER SQUID

The vampire squid lives up to 10,000 ft (3,050 m) below the ocean surface and gets its name from its dark, webbed arms, which it can draw over itself like Dracula's cloak.

CRAZY FOR CHROMATICS

A three-year-old feline named Olive in Derbyshire, England, has taken multicolored eyes to the next level.

The physical condition occurs in cats, dogs, and even people and is characterized by different colored eyes. But Olive is a truly unique individual because she has sectoral heterochromia. This means the iris of each eye is divided into two colors. In the case of Olive, her blue and yellow eyes are so stunning that photos of her have gone viral.

THE ZOMBIE SNAIL!

THE STALKING DEAD

The parasitic *Leucochloridium* flatworm invades the bodies of snails and turns them into zombies, forcing the snail to move into open areas where they will get eaten by birds!

The twisted life cycle of the flatworm starts as an egg inside bird droppings. When a snail eats the droppings, the flatworm hatches and compels the snail to move into an open area. The worm then crawls into the snail's eyestalk and begins pulsating and flashing bright colors to attract birds. When a bird finally eats the worm-snail combo, the worm releases eggs into the bird's intestines, which get pooped out to begin the cycle again.

Ripley's Exhibit

Cat. No. 174562

Paper Chain

A 25-mi-long (40.2-km) paper chain created by Butch Baker of Four Oaks, North Carolina. Starting in 1979, Butch added to the paper chain for more than 40 years!

Believe it or not, there are Ripley's brochures making up portions of the chain!

25 MI (40.2 KM) OF PAPER CHAIN!

inside the vault

As a pile, the paper chain was too large to go through doors, so it had to be strung single-file onto spools through a window.

Here Butch stands where he kept the chain piled up in his home. Note the new paint and carpet where he had to work around the paper behemoth.

43-FT (13-M) PAPER DRAGON!

FOLDED FIRE-BREATHER

To commemorate the final season of HBO's *Game of Thrones*, a UK-based stationary supplier crafted a 43-ft-long (13-m) freestanding paper sculpture of a dragon using 1,200 sheets of paper.

The stationary supplier, Viking Direct, hired Andy Singleton to create the fire-breathing behemoth. It took him more than 100 studio hours and 10 hours of installation before the project was complete. Made entirely from carefully cut and scored paper, the sculpture relied on minimal wooden supports to achieve its breathtaking height. Viking Direct donated the sculpture to a local school once the last episode of *Game of Thrones* aired.

CACTUS TATTOO
Around 2,000 years ago, tattoo artists in North America pigmented people's skin by using a pen-sized wooden tool fitted with cactus spines.

TOUGH WATCH
Robert Bainter lost his Apple Watch while body surfing in the ocean at Huntington Beach, California, and when it was found and returned to him six months later, it still worked.

GRAY UNIFORMS
The tradition of visiting baseball teams wearing gray uniforms dates back to the 19th century when traveling teams did not have time to launder their uniforms and so they wore gray to conceal the dirt.

METEORITE DOORSTOP
An object that a man had been using as a barn doorstop on his farm in Edmore, Michigan, for more than 30 years turned out to be a meteorite worth $100,000.

SHOCKING RETURN
Aigali Supugaliev, 63, returned to his home village of Tomarly, Kazakhstan, in 2018—two months after his family thought they had buried him. After he had been reported missing, a decomposed corpse was found close to his home, and when a DNA test found a 99.92 percent chance that the body was his, he was given a solemn funeral. Instead, he had been working away on a distant farm for four months but had neglected to inform his relatives.

Light It Up
During an eruption of the Ebeko volcano in Russia, German photographer Martin Reitze captured volcanic lightning. One of the rarest phenomena in nature, Reitze stood less than a mile from the event. Over the past two centuries, volcanic lightning has been documented at approximately 200 eruptions. But researchers often chase the phenomenon for a decade or more before witnessing it firsthand, much less getting a photo.

WET BABIES
Human babies are about the same percentage of water as a banana. A newborn baby is 75 percent water, compared to a banana's 74 percent.

UNEXPLODED SHELLS
Almost 50 tons of unexploded World War I shells are recovered every year from the battlefield near Verdun in Northern France. It may be hundreds of years before the last of the millions of shells that were fired over 10 months in 1916 are removed.

A 12-lb (5.5-kg) lunar meteorite sold for more than $600,000 in 2018. The piece of Moon rock had crashed to Earth in Mauritania, Africa, the previous year.

FIRST SHOES
Famous fashion designer Jimmy Choo made his first pair of shoes at age 11—a pair of leather slippers for his mom's birthday.

FRENCH VOICE
Ellen Spencer, from Indianapolis, Indiana, has been speaking with a mysterious French accent for more than 10 years, but it disappears when she sings. She developed the condition, known as foreign accent syndrome, following a series of head injuries.

TOY TRAIN

In 1936, Robert Ripley discovered the "Toy Train" in India, a diminutive 2-ft (0.6-m) gauge railway running next to buildings and markets, and it's still chugging today.

Part of the Mountain Railways of India, the Darjeeling Himalayan Railway (DHR) runs between New Jalpaiguri and Darjeeling, climbing 6,890 ft (2,100 m) en route. The track stretches 55 mi (88.5 km), with five loops and six zigzags to accommodate the ascent. Six diesel locomotives handle daily services. Steam train enthusiasts have the option of taking the Red Panda, a toy train that travels from Darjeeling to Kurseong along the DHR and is powered by British-built, B-class steam locomotives. UNESCO declared the DHR a World Heritage Site in 1999.

2-FT-WIDE (0.6-M) TRACK

Robert Ripley's 1936 visit to India left quite the impression on him. He featured much of what he saw in the Believe It or Not! cartoon, including the Darjeeling Himalayan Railway, proclaiming it to be "The Crookedest Railroad in the World."

58,000

The number of speeding drivers caught on temporary cameras in less than two weeks in the Italian village of Acquetico—despite the town having just 120 residents.

SNAIL RAIL
It is illegal to carry live snails on a French high-speed train unless they have a ticket.

PADDLE COMMUTER
To save a one-hour drive to work in Chongqing, China, insurance agent Liu Fucao paddleboards across the Yangtze River, cutting his journey time to just six minutes.

SQUIRREL LASAGNA
One of the specialty dishes of Ivan Tisdall-Downes, chef at London, England, restaurant Native, is gray-squirrel lasagna.

STRANGE SIGNAL
Tipperary Hill in Syracuse, New York, has an upside-down traffic signal with the red light below the green—instead of the other way around.

TOURIST HAVEN
Three times as many tourists (33 million) visit Greece each year than the entire population of the country (10.7 million).

LAST SPEAKERS
There are believed to be only two remaining speakers of Ter Sámi, a language traditionally spoken in Russia's Kola Peninsula. There were about 450 at the end of the 19th century.

FIRE AND ICE
Close to the Bandera volcano in New Mexico, where red-hot lava flowed in a spectacular eruption 10,000 years ago, is an ice cave in which the temperature never rises above freezing. The 75-ft-deep (23-m) cave is located in a section of collapsed lava tube, and at the bottom of the cave, the ice is 20 ft (6 m) thick.

BABY UNIT
Traffic is so bad in Bangkok, Thailand, that the police department has a special unit for delivering babies for mothers who don't make it to the hospital in time. Since the unit was set up in 1987, Bangkok's traffic police have delivered more than 100 babies. In 2018, Police Captain Pichet Wisetchok helped deliver his 33rd baby.

BLOOD SOUP
The Spartans of ancient Greece served a black soup made of salt, vinegar, and pigs' blood. The vinegar prevented the blood from clotting during cooking.

TOOTH MOUSE
Instead of the tooth fairy, when a child loses a tooth in Spain, a small mouse called Ratoncito Pérez traditionally leaves a surprise gift under the pillow.

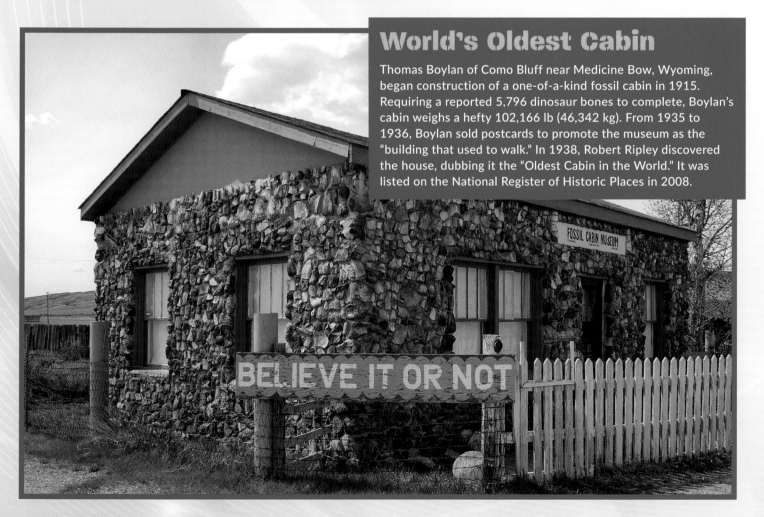

World's Oldest Cabin
Thomas Boylan of Como Bluff near Medicine Bow, Wyoming, began construction of a one-of-a-kind fossil cabin in 1915. Requiring a reported 5,796 dinosaur bones to complete, Boylan's cabin weighs a hefty 102,166 lb (46,342 kg). From 1935 to 1936, Boylan sold postcards to promote the museum as the "building that used to walk." In 1938, Robert Ripley discovered the house, dubbing it the "Oldest Cabin in the World." It was listed on the National Register of Historic Places in 2008.

SEASON'S CREEPINGS

In Wales, nothing says Christmas like a visit from a rhyme-spouting dead horse.

Some holiday traditions transcend the cultural divide. There's the Christmas tree, originally from Germany, and Santa Claus, based on a historical figure from Turkey. The Welsh Mari Lwyd, however, doesn't translate well at all. A pagan tradition that predates Christianity, the horse skull-headed figure haunts the yuletide. The costumed creature beckons people to engage him in epic *pwnco* poetry battles. Losers have to let the terrifying creature inside for food and drink.

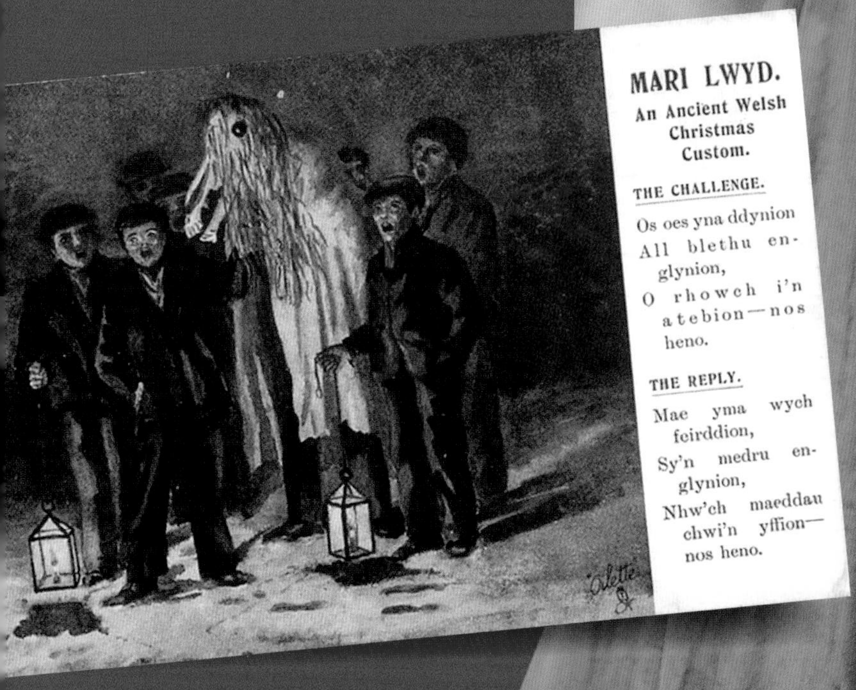

MARI LWYD.
An Ancient Welsh Christmas Custom.

THE CHALLENGE.

Os oes yna ddynion
All blethu en-
glynion,
O rhowch i'n
atebion—nos
heno.

THE REPLY.

Mae yma wych
feirddion,
Sy'n medru en-
glynion,
Nhw'ch maeddau
chwi'n yffion—
nos heno.

Treelieve It or Not!

A Christmas-tree-obsessed couple in northwestern Germany has brought new meaning to the phrase "deck the halls." How? By filling their home with 350 decorated trees—even in the bathroom! They start putting the trees up in September and spend eight weeks decorating. Creations include red-and-white snowman-themed trees and others covered in fruity ornaments.

CHAINSAW HORROR

Bill Singleton, a 68-year-old from Victoria, Australia, drove himself 15 mi (25 km) to the hospital after accidentally cutting his face and tongue in half with a chainsaw. He had been cutting wood when he lost control of his saw, causing it to ricochet into his face. He was unable to call for help because he had sliced through his own tongue, and so he had to crawl to his car and seek urgent medical attention. Surgeons said he was 0.4 in (1 cm) from severing his carotid artery, which would almost certainly have killed him.

ISLAND DISGUISE

During World War II, the Dutch warship *Abraham Crijnssen* was disguised as a tropical island to escape being detected by the Japanese fleet. Covered in trees and branches and kept anchored and immobile close to shore during daylight hours, it was the only ship of its class to survive in the seas around Java.

DESSERT TOWER

Hyakusho Udon, a store in Miyazaki Prefecture, Japan, serves shaved ice desserts that are more than 2 ft (0.6 m) tall and can only be eaten standing up. The 634-mm-tall tower is inspired by the 634-m-tall (2,080-ft) Tokyo Skytree building.

Log Surprise

Move over, Elf on the Shelf! In the Catalan region of Spain, families keep a Caga Tió, or Tió de Nadal, a log decorated like an elf that "poops" nougat underneath a blanket when fed food scraps and then beaten with a stick. Caga Tió can appear in many shapes and sizes, from massive tree trunks in the middle of a town square to smaller versions for inside the home.

PILLOW FIGHTS

Pillow fighting is now a serious sport in Japan. Two teams of five line up on opposing mats and hurl pillows at each other, the object being to hit the opposing team's designated king with a pillow. One player on each team is allowed to brandish a defensive duvet to block oncoming pillows.

FIRST PIZZA

After the forces under Italian dictator Benito Mussolini held her husband hostage during World War II, Audrey Prudence, from Essex, England, refused to eat any Italian food for 74 years—until in 2019, at age 94, when she finally relented and ate a Hawaiian pizza.

EXPLORER'S REMAINS

The remains of English explorer Captain Matthew Flinders (1774–1814), the first person to circumnavigate Australia and identify it as a continent, were discovered buried beneath London's Euston train station in 2019.

PIZZA CRAZY

Mike Roman, a teacher from Hackensack, New Jersey, has eaten pizza for dinner every day for four decades—and often for lunch, too. He started his pizza diet at age four and has since consumed in the vicinity of 15,000 pizzas.

ALWAYS LOOKING UP!

These snakes have found a unique way to adapt to life in the arid deserts of the Arabian Peninsula—eyes on the top of their heads.

Arabian sand boas can grow to about 16 in (41 cm) in length. Their flat noses work like tiny shovels to help them disappear into the sand without a trace. The peculiar location of their eyes lets them scope out their surroundings without baking in the sun. As a result, they can spend searing desert days buried almost entirely in the sand, unseen and ready to ambush prey.

Pollywog Party

A scuba diver and underwater photographer from British Columbia, Canada, recently captured extraordinary images while swimming with hundreds of tadpoles. Maxwel Hohn captured the breathtaking scene while on Vancouver Island. To get the perfect images, Hohn lay on the bottom of the shallow lake among the algae and water plants, waiting for the massive gathering to arrive. To protect the lake and its extraordinary inhabitants from over-tourism, Hohn has not disclosed the name of the lake on social media. But his images remain a potent witness to the event.

DOUBLE AGENT

Spanish double agent Juan Pujol Garcia received military honors from both sides during World War II. Garcia, who secretly worked against Nazi Germany and played an important role in the success of D-Day, was awarded the Iron Cross by the Germans and was also made a Member of the Order of the British Empire by the British. He was given the codename "Garbo" by the British and "Alaric" by the Germans.

When humans search for computer files, they use the same part of the brain that a dog uses when looking for a bone.

STOMACH NEEDLES

Raziye Yildrim, from Izmir, Turkey, was shocked to learn that she had been living with a pair of 2-in-long (5-cm) needles in her stomach for 66 years. She remembered pushing three needles into her stomach when she was two years old, but it turned out that surgeons only removed one at the time. It was only six decades later when she was hospitalized with abdominal pain that the remaining needles were discovered and removed.

FrankenCar

Measuring 10.4 ft (3.2 m) tall, 8.2 ft (2.5 m) wide, and 35.4 ft (10.8 m) long, this one-of-a-kind vehicle weighs an astonishing 24 tons, making it the largest SUV in the world. Known as the "Dhabiyan," the bespoke SUV was crafted for car collector Sheikh Hamad bin Hamdan Al Nahyan. Featuring parts from a Dodge Dart, a Jeep Wrangler, and an Oshkosh M1075 military truck, the ten-wheeled behemoth dominates on- and off-road.

JUMBO
WATER FIGHT

Every April in Ayutthaya, Thailand, locals, tourists, and even elephants take part in the world's biggest water fight!

Whether by counting down the ball drop or watching fireworks, cultures around the world ring in the new year differently. But Songkran (Thai New Year) takes the cake when it comes to unique festivities. Beginning on April 13 and lasting for a few days, Songkran has been dubbed the world's biggest water fight, as everybody from water gun–wielding locals and tourists to painted elephants with refill buckets get involved. Not only does frolicking in water prove fun, but it's thought to wash away bad luck according to the Thai culture.

Buddhist Android

At the dimly lit Kodaiji Zen Temple in Kyoto, Japan, Buddhist monks gather around Mindar—an android-version of Kannon, the goddess of mercy. She cost an estimated 100 million yen ($909,090) to construct and teaches Buddhist philosophy. Programmed to recite part of the Heart Sutras, she speaks in Japanese while Chinese and English translations appear on a nearby screen. A collaborative effort by the temple and Hiroshi Ishiguro, a professor of intelligent robotics at Osaka University, they hope Mindar will attract a younger crowd to Buddhism.

Glowing Grotto

Discovered in the 1830s by a hunter, the Cave Saint-Marcel-d'Ardèche in France contains an impressive 35-mi-long (57-km) expanse of tunnels and chambers. Descending into the cave is like entering another universe. At a steady temperature of 57°F (14°C) year-round, the cave is filled with natural geologic features, including stalactites, stalagmites, and artificially illuminated calcite pools. It also boasts prehistoric artwork that will make you feel as if you've stepped back in time.

PINBALL PROHIBITION

Pinball machines were banned in New York City from 1942 to 1976 because they were thought to be a game of chance and therefore a form of gambling. So pinball prohibition lasted more than twice as long as alcohol prohibition (1920–1933).

ICY BET

Every winter in Newport, Vermont, local people take part in the ICE OUT contest to guess and bet on how long the ice will last on Lake Memphremagog. To determine the exact time the ice melts, a weighted mascot is placed on the ice with a clock. Once the ice beneath it gives way, the exact time is used to square up the bet—the person who guessed the closest date and time without going over wins a cash prize.

Up to $2,800

The fine for anyone caught hiking in flip-flops at Cinque Terre National Park in Italy.

SHOE FENCE

A shoe fence more than 150 ft (50 m) long borders State Highway 6 near Havelock on New Zealand's South Island. It was started more than 20 years ago as a practical joke and now consists of hundreds of discarded shoes, sneakers, and boots.

BIRTHDAY LAW

In Tajikistan, it is illegal to celebrate your birthday in public or with anyone other than family members. Tajik pop star Firuza Hafizova was fined $530 for celebrating her birthday at home with friends in 2018.

HUGE DAM

The amount of concrete used to build the 643-ft-high (196-m) hydroelectric Itaipu Dam on the Paraná River on the border of Paraguay and Brazil could have built 210 football stadiums. The dam's reservoir covers an area of 520 sq mi (1,350 sq km)—more than twice the size of Chicago.

Ripley's Exhibit

Cat. No. 5249

Whale Barnacles

Barnacle parasites that
cling to whales.

Ripley's Exhibit

Cat. No. 5126

Headhunter Statue

Mahogany carving of an Igorot headhunter
with a decapitated head in his left hand.

inside the vault

Ripley's Exhibit

Cat. No. 5410

Clothespin Clock

1930s grandfather clock made from more than 3,000 ordinary clothespins. Created by Victor Lundberg.

MORE THAN 3,000 CLOTHESPINS!

Point of View

Unveiled in London's iconic Borough Market in 2019, artist Michael Murphy's portrait of Dolly Raheema, a trash picker from Bengaluru, India, is composed of 1,500 scavenged plastic parts suspended from the ceiling with fishing line. When observed from the side, these parts appear to have no order or pattern. But when viewed from the front, they create a multilayered, three-dimensional portrait of Raheema. The portrait celebrates a new initiative by The Body Shop to use recycled plastic and support marginalized trash pickers in India.

STREET SALMON
When the Skokomish River overflowed in Shelton, Washington, in November 2018, large salmon from the river were seen swimming across the nearby flooded U.S. Highway 101.

BIRTH BAN
An ancient tradition forbids children from being born in the village of Mafi Dove, Ghana. Instead, heavily pregnant women are transported to neighboring villages and may only return once they have given birth.

SAUSAGE HOTEL
Butcher Claus Boebel has opened a sausage-themed hotel—the Boebel Bratwurst Bed and Breakfast—in Rittersbach, Germany. The rooms have sausage-shaped pillows, a bratwurst design on the wallpaper, and sausage decorations hanging from the ceiling. Among the items on the hotel menu is sausage-flavored ice cream.

KEY CROPS
Of the 6,000 plant species that are cultivated for food, just nine—sugarcane, maize, rice, wheat, potatoes, soybeans, oil-palm fruit, sugar beet, and cassava—account for two-thirds of the world's total crop production.

CHEESY MUSIC
A Swiss cheesemaker discovered that exposing the popular food to hip-hop music gives it more flavor. Cheesemaker Beat Wampfler spent six months playing different types of music—ranging from Led Zeppelin to Mozart—to eight wheels of his Emmental cheese, and hip-hop produced the best results.

DIFFERENT TIMES
The town of Cameron Corner straddles the border of three Australian states with three different time zones. So the New Year is rung in three times in the town, each half an hour apart—first New South Wales, then South Australia, and finally Queensland.

LIE DETECTOR
Some Bedouin tribes in northeastern Egypt still practice the Bisha'h, an ancient lie detector test in which suspects are forced to lick a red-hot spoon in the presence of tribal leaders. If their tongue blisters, they are found guilty; if it is unharmed, they are proven innocent.

VAMPIRE TEETH
Yaeba, or crooked teeth, are considered attractive in Japan, prompting some girls to go to the dentist to have their upper canine teeth deliberately shaped so that they resemble vampire fangs.

CARDBOARD CRUISIN'

Each July, residents of Bideford, England, take to the River Torridge in homemade cardboard boats.

The aptly titled Bideford Cardboard Boat Regatta brings out teams and individuals to participate. Propelling their self-made cardboard vessels, they must pass two buoy turns before paddling back to their origin point, Kingsley Steps. Along the way, plenty of cardboard boat carnage occurs. Many upcycled boats capsize, sink, or flat-out disintegrate. Prizes get awarded in a variety of categories, including best submarine, slowest boat, and the most entertaining capsize.

✉ FAN FEED

Lost and Found!

Debi of Davenport, Florida, wrote us with the remarkable story of her 12-year-old dog, Marley, who went missing for seven months. According to rescuers, Marley lived in a snake-infested fenced-in corner by the busy Interstate-4 Highway and a Holiday Inn Express parking lot. While fending for himself, he ate food scavenged from the garbage and boxes of takeout contributed by guests of the hotel. His water came from a nearby truck-washing station. As Debi notes, "It is truly a miracle he survived."

HAPPY AND HEALTHY AGAIN!

Frog Wedding

On June 8, 2019, residents of Udupi, Karnataka, India held a Mandooka Parinaya (marriage of frogs) to appease the rain gods and end their region's drought. Caught from neighboring villages, the frogs were carefully inspected by the Department of Zoology in Manipal before being christened Varuna (the god of water) and Varsha (rain). Wedding invitations were sent, traditional wedding garments were tailored for the warty duo, and a honeymoon was organized in the neighboring village of Mannapalla. The ceremony may have been too effective—just a couple months later, the region began experiencing floods!

I DO!

NO SNOUT ABOUT IT

Bonnie the border collie mix was found as a puppy near a railway track in Romania with part of her nose and front left leg missing, but she's made a miraculous recovery!

Now she lives in the UK with Kate and Ross Comfort, who adopted Bonnie after seeing her on a social media post from the Beacon Animal Rescue Centre. She was having trouble finding a forever home, but the Comforts fell in love with her immediately. Her facial and leg injuries have healed and do not affect her day-to-day happiness. And while Bonnie doesn't look like your typical dog, that hasn't stopped more than 20,000 people from following her on Instagram!

TOE-BITERS

Giant water bugs devour fish, frogs, turtles, and even snakes by sucking them to death from the inside!

The bug clamps onto its prey with its strong legs before injecting it with digestive juices that break down its body from the inside out. The insect then sucks out the victim's dissolving insides through its straw-like mouth. By this method, the 4-in-long (10-cm) bugs can eat prey up to 10 times their own size!

Lucky for us, various species of these big bugs can be found in fresh water around the world, including where humans live, and will attack just about anything that moves in front of them, giving them the nickname "toe-biters." The bite is extremely painful for humans.

BABY BUGS!

The females of some toe-biter species will attach their eggs to the backs of males, where the offspring will stay until hatched.

The giant water bug is an ambush predator, hiding perfectly still in vegetation while it waits for a meal to swim by and then—SNAP!

ACTUAL SIZE!

Weird Roommates

This cute wood duckling was raised by an eastern screech owl, one of its natural predators! Wood ducks don't put all their eggs in one basket—females are "brood parasites" and lay their eggs in different nests so other mothers can raise the hatchlings. Found in artist and photographer Laurie Wolf's backyard, this chick hatched a month after the owl moved into the nesting box. After calling for her parents, the wood duckling suddenly jumped out of the box and made a beeline for the nearest body of water.

This "parasitic" nesting behavior is also found in the cuckoo bird. Once hatched, the cuckoo chick pushes the other eggs or hatchlings out of the nest to commandeer space and food.

Malaysian pen-tailed tree shrews live on a diet of fermented nectar, but despite drinking the equivalent of a dozen glasses of wine each night, they never appear drunk.

PARROT LINGUIS

Lubomir Michna was able to show that he was the rightful owner of Hugo, an African gray parrot found at Dublin Airport in Ireland, by proving that the bird speaks Slovak. Four people had come forward to claim Hugo, but the parrot only reacted excitedly when it heard Slovak voice recordings.

FIRST SIGHTING

The Fernandina giant tortoise was rediscovered in 2019—more than a century after it was thought to have become extinct. A female was found on the Galápagos island of Fernandina off the coast of Ecuador, the first confirmed sighting of the species since 1906.

HORROR INSECT

The female parasitic conopid fly attacks bumblebees in midair and injects an egg, which, two days later, hatches into a larva that proceeds to eat the still living bee from the inside. The larva then forces the bee to land on the ground and dig a hole as its own grave. The parasite continues to grow inside the dead bee and eventually bursts out of the corpse as a mature fly ready to attack more bumblebees.

140

The number of species of land snakes in Australia—including 100 venomous snakes—but note there are none in neighboring New Zealand.

1.5 M

The number of Adélie penguins in a supercolony on the Danger Islands around Antarctica that were discovered thanks to their pink poop stains, which are visible from space.

10,000

The number of pet bees a couple kept on the balcony of their high-rise apartment in Ningbo, China, for more than a year to develop a bee sting treatment for relieving painful conditions such as rheumatoid arthritis.

BLOAT 'N' FLOAT

When they want to move to a new location, sea cucumbers fill their bodies with water until they become bloated and buoyant, detach themselves from the ocean floor, and then float off with the current.

TOILET SHOCK

Helen Richards was bitten on the butt by a python while she sat on the toilet in her home in Chapel Hill, Queensland, Australia.

DOG DETECTIVE

In his five years as a sniffer dog in Wales, Scamp the English springer spaniel has detected nearly $8 million worth of illegal tobacco. He is so good, in fact, that he had to stop working in one area of the country because an organized crime group placed a $32,617 (£25,000) bounty on his head!

ZOMBIE SPIDER

The Amazon River wasp lays its eggs on the abdomen of a spider and then invades its brain, turning the spider into a zombie. The wasp hijacks the arachnid's nervous system, forcing it to leave its colony, protect the wasp's larvae, and eventually get eaten alive.

GOLF SPRINT

Former Major League Baseball star Eric Byrnes played 420 holes of golf in 24 hours at Half Moon Bay Golf Links in California. Starting at 7:00 a.m. on April 22, 2019, and playing through the night, he used just one club, walked 106 mi (170 km), and took a total of 3,438 strokes. His lowest round score was 116, and his was highest 168.

AIRPORT LIMBO

While waiting at Philadelphia International Airport for a flight to her home in Buffalo, New York, Shemika Campbell bent her body backward and performed a limbo in the tiny space beneath the seats in the departure lounge. Her flexibility runs in the family, as both her mother and grandmother were also limbo dancers.

RUNNING BACKWARD

New York Mets baseball player Jimmy Piersall celebrated his 100th career home run—against the Philadelphia Phillies on June 23, 1963—by running the bases in the correct order but facing backward. On another occasion, he stepped up to bat wearing a Beatles wig and playing air guitar on his bat.

BEARDED BATTLEMASTER

Not only does Rose Geil sport a beard, but she competes against all-male rivals and almost always wins!

After spending more than 20 years shaving twice a day and carrying a razor in her purse, Rose decided to embrace radical self-love. This meant not only letting her facial hair grow, but even participating in beard contests. Quickly earning a reputation as a crowd pleaser and judge favorite, she attributes her success to being the only woman with a natural beard in the room.

WOMEN SCIENTISTS

While you've heard of Marie Curie, her daughter Irène Curie-Joliot also won a Nobel Prize in chemistry in 1935, making them the first parent-child pair to receive Nobel Prizes independently.

Elizabeth Blackwell graduated first in her class from the Geneva Medical College in 1849, becoming the first woman to receive a medical degree in the United States. She went on to found a school of medicine for women in New York and advocate for poor women's health.

In 1992, Mae C. Jemison, a medical doctor who served with the Peace Corps in Sierra Leone, became the first African American female astronaut, as a crew member on the spaceship *Endeavour*.

SIDESHOW SCIENCE

StrongWomen Science blends magic and science to create spellbinding performances!

Scientists Maria Corcoran and Aoife Raleigh recently took the Edinburgh Science Festival by storm with their breathtaking StrongWomen Science act. Maria and Aoife performed a variety of circus acts. Then, they revealed the secrets behind each stunt, from fire eating to acrobatics, hula-hoop performances to juggling. They even offered post-show, hands-on activities to let audience members in on the act.

Chinese American particle physicist Sau Lan Wu won the Nobel Prize in physics in 1963 and has made three groundbreaking discoveries: charm quarks, gluons, and the Higgs boson particle.

Hollywood heartthrob Hedy Lamarr pioneered transmitting radio signals via changing frequencies to ensure American radio-guided weapons remained undetected during WWII.

92
U

Despite facing prejudice as a Jewish woman in mid-20th-century Austria, Lise Meitner discovered that uranium atoms split when bombarded with neutrons—the phenomenon of "nuclear fission."

WOMEN SCIENTISTS

Ripley's Exhibit

Cat. No. 18848

Camel Bone Carving

Camel bone carving of gods on a mountain. Designed by Xie Man Hua of Guangzou, China, this camel bone carving depicts Sun Wukong's defiance of the gods and is called "The Monkey Mountain." Believe it or not, it took 40 carvers more than six months to complete!

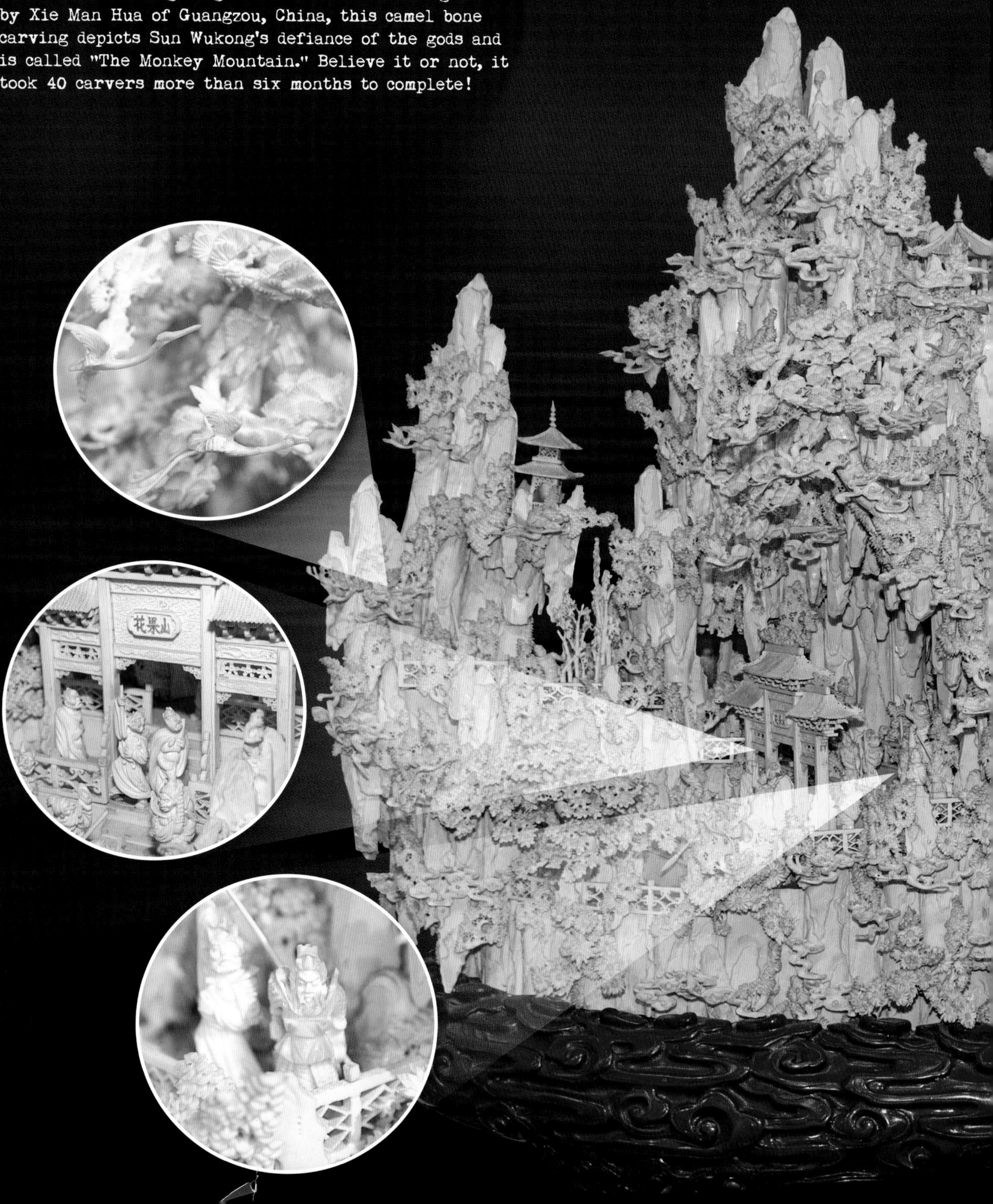

inside the vault

花果山

INDEX

Page numbers in italic refer to images.

ACKNOWLEDGMENTS

4 (bl) Photography by Colton Kruse, (br) Photos courtesy of Gina Keller/Brian Backland (Photographer) and Brenda Mullins (Seamstress); 5 (tl) Courtesy of Alain Sainz, (c) Photography by Steph Distasio, (b) Courtesy of Christopher Horsley; 6 (bl) Colorized by Luis Fuentes; 7 (b) Courtesy of Charles and Allie Trippy; 11 (tl, tr) Illustrated by John Graziano; 12–13 (t) Photography by Steve Campbell and Matt Mamula; 13 (br) Created by Rose Audette; 14 Edwin Remsberg/VWPics via AP Images; 15 (r, bl) AFP via Getty Images; 16–19 Courtesy of Christopher Horsley; 22 (t) Dr. Hubert Zitt/Cover Images, (b) University of Queensland/Cover Images; 23 (t, br) Serghei Pakhomoff/Caters News; 24 (t) Andrei Gilbert/Alamy Stock Photo, (tl) Frank Lennon/Toronto Star via Getty Images, (b) Owe Andersson/Alamy Stock Photo; 25 (tr) © Startbosshogg, Wikimedia Commons // CC-BY-SA 4.0; 26 (t) Supplied by WENN.com via Cover Images; 27 (sp) CARROT LIM/ CATERS NEWS; 28 (bl, br) Shiraaz Mohamed/Gallo Images/Getty Images; 28–29 (dps) Shiraaz Mohamed/Gallo Images/Getty Images; 30 (t, b) BEN VON WONG/CATERS; 31 AirPano. com/Solent News; 32 (t, b) Courtesy of Emerald Downs; 33 (tr, c) Michael Scott/Caters News; 34 (t) Courtesy of Stina Nyberg, (b) National Weather Service via AP/Shutterstock; 35 Northern Territory Parks and Wildlife Commission; 38 (tr, cr, bl, br) Caters News; 39 Benoit Sabourin/ CATERS NEWS; 40 (t, cr, bl, br) SCHWEINE MUSEUM/CATERS NEWS; 41 (tl, tr, br) Courtesy of Kristie Wolf; 42–43 Photos courtesy of Big Thing Small Town TM; 44 (t) William Stevenson via Getty, (t) Alex Schwab via Getty Images, (b) © jamie.sue.photography/Shutterstock.com; 45 (t, b) © Jugoslav Belada/Solent News & Photo Agency; 46 (t) Scott Sady/tahoelight.com/Alamy Stock Photo, (b) Stephanie Sampson IG/FB @thevanlifechronicles; 47 (t) MICHAL CIZEK/AFP via Getty Images; 48 (t) Emanuele Biggi/naturepl.com, (c) © Karen N. Pelletreau et al., Wikimedia Commons//CC-BY-SA 4.0; 49 Courtesy of Melissa Davis; 50–51 (b) Schafer & Hill via Getty Images; 51 (tr) National Geographic Image Collection/Alamy Stock Photo; 54–55 Photography by Steph Distasio; 56 Courtesy of John Farnworth; 57 (tr, br) Photography by Steph Distasio; 58 (sp, br) Courtesy of John Grade; 59 (t) Ravikanth Kurma/Shutterstock; 60 The Asahi Shimbun via Getty Images; 61 (t, c) The Asahi Shimbun via Getty Images; 62–63 (b) The Asahi Shimbun via Getty Images; 63 (br) Courtesy of Dawn Saavedra; 64–65 Courtesy of Unneccessary Inventions, www.unnecessaryinventions.com; 66 (sp, br) McMaster University/Cover Images; 67 (t) Homer Sykes/Alamy Stock Photo, (b) Eduardo Blanco via Nature Picture Library; 68 (tl, tr, bl, br) PATRICIA CASTELLANOS/AFP via Getty Images; 69 © UK Kurochanup/Shutterstock.com; 70 (b) © Wellcome Library no. 644751i, Wikimedia Commons//CC-BY-SA 4.0; 72 (t) Public Domain {{PD-US}}, (tr) Public Domain {{PD-US}} Fox Photos/Hulton Archive. Fotograf nicht namentlich bekannt, (b) REUTERS/Pascal Rossignol; 73 Masayoshi Matsumoto; 74–75 Photo by Thibaud Moritz/Abaca/Sipa USA(Sipa via AP Images); 75 (tr) GEORGES GOBET/AFP via Getty Images, (cr) Photo by Thibaud Moritz/Abaca/Sipa USA (Sipa via AP Images); 76 Courtesy of Adam Uttendaal; 77 (t) Courtesy of Doc Jon; 78 (sp, b) BORIS HORVAT/ AFP/Getty Images; 79 (t, b) Courtesy of Barry Osborn; 80 (c, b) Dennis Cox/Alamy Stock Photo; 81 (tl, tc, tr, bl, br) © McLeod , Wikimedia Commons//CC-BY-SA 3.0, (b) MIGUEL GUTIERREZ/AFP/Getty Images; 82 (t, b) MARIO VAZQUEZ/AFP/Getty Images; 83 (tr) Mark Graves/The Oregonian via AP, (b) Courtesy of Sean Oulashin and Matt Leonetti; 84–85 Courtesy of Philip Vance; 86–87 (bkg) Terry Whittaker/naturepl.com; 87 (tl) blickwinkel/Alamy Stock Photo, (tr, bc) Terry Whittaker/naturepl.com; 90 (cl, tr) Courtesy of Christina Vogel; 91 (br, bl, cr) Caters News; 92 (t, bl, br) @rainbowroadtrip/Caters News; 93 (tl, tr) LOIC VENANCE/AFP/Getty Images, (bl, br) @rainbowroadtrip/Caters News; 94 (t, b) ULISES RUIZ/AFP/Getty Images; 95 (t) Courtesy of J.R. Majewski; 96–97 Photography by Colton Kruse; 98 Courtesy of LadyBEAST; 99 (t) Courtesy of LadyBEAST, (r) Photography by Colton Kruse; 100 (t) Photo courtesy of Elliot Sumner, (bc, br) Savannah Boan/CATERS NEWS; 101 Courtesy of Mac's Mission/macsmission.org; 102 (t, r) PA Images/Alamy Stock Photo; 102–103 (bkg) ANDY BUCHANAN/AFP/Getty Images; 103 (tl) Colin McPherson/Alamy Stock Photo; 104 (t, b, sp) Mercury Press & Media/Caters News; 105 (t) Caters News, (b) Ajay Verma/Barcroft India/Barcroft Media via Getty Images; 108–109 Courtesy of Sam Barsky; 110–111 Courtesy of Brian Delaurenti and Johnathan Dahl; 112 (t) Courtesy of Juan Javier Carrasco Alcedo; 113 (sp, bl) ADAM HILLMAN/ CATERS NEWS; 114 (dps) Tuul and Bruno Morandi/Alamy Stock Photo; 115 (c) © Wang Ji, Wikimedia Commons//CC-BY 2.5; 116 (t, BL) Mercury Press/Caters News; 117 (tl) Caters News, (tr) MisFitt/Alamy Stock Photo; 118 (l) Public Domain {{PD-US}}, (r) Courtesy of Taylor Valdés; 119 James D. Morgan/Getty Images; 120–121 FallingInSand.com; 122 Courtesy of Zion Martyn; 123 (t) Finley Molloy, Instagram: Finnyboymolloy, (b) Courtesy of Julius Dalsgaard Bertelsen/The Floo Network; 124 Photos courtesy of Michael Aquilina @aquamike23 on Instagram and Leonel Junior Justiniano – photographer; 125 (t) Rahul Sachdev/Caters News, (b) Courtesy of Cyril Ruoso; 128 (t) CATERS NEWS, (b) Fernando Sette/CATERS NEWS; 129 (t, br) CATERS NEWS; 130–131 Courtesy of Quitterie Ithurbide; 132 Kristian Laine//kristianlainephotography, www.kristianlainephotography.com; 133 (t) J—M/LAMAN Tim via Nature Picture Library, (b) Paul Williams via Nature Picture Library; 134 (cl) Brian Overcast/Alamy Stock Photo, (bc) © Francisco Anzola, Flickr Creative Commons//CC-BY 2.0, (br) © Michael Lubinski, Flickr Creative Commons // CC-BY 2.0; 134–135 (b) Public Domain {{PD-US}}; 135 (bl) © Kaethe17, Wikimedia Commons//CC-BY-SA 4.0, (bc) © Ralf Roletschek/roletschek.at, licensed under the terms of the GNU Free Documentation License, Version 1.2, (br) Martchan/Alamy Stock Photo; 136 James Bruton, YouTube Channel, youtube.com/jamesbruton; 137 (t) Photo by Harry Shepherd/Fox Photos/Hulton Archive/Getty Images; (b) Ruslan Kalnitsky/Alamy Stock Photo; 138 (t) Arcaid Images/Alamy Stock Photo, (r) Jakub Dvořák/Alamy Stock Photo; 139 China Photos/Getty Images; 142–143 Courtesy of Kelvin Wiley; 144 (t) Chesnot/Getty Images, (br) STR/AFP via Getty Images, (b) Mercury Stock Photo; 145 (t) STR/AFP via Getty Images, (b) Marcos Ruiz Ceballos, a circus artist from Spain; 146 (tr) Ken Welsh/Education Images/Universal Images Group via Getty Images, (b) WENN Rights Ltd/Alamy Stock Photo; 147 (t) Public Domain CC0 1.0 Universal (CC0 1.0), (bc) Photo by Matt Cardy/Getty Images, (br) Rick Colls/Alamy Stock Photo; 148 (b) © Steve Hopkin/ardea.com; 148–149 (dps) coward_lion/Alamy Stock Photo; 149 (t) Image navi - QxQ images/Alamy Stock Photo; 150 Courtesy of Trace Wilson; 151 (t) Photography by Steve Campbell and Matt Mamula; 152 (bl) Perry Svensson/Alamy; 152–153 (dp) Billy H.C. Kwok/Getty Images; 154 (sp) Steffen Trumpf/picture alliance via Getty Images, (cl) yardbirdstock.com/Alamy Stock Photo, (b) Steffen Trumpf/picture alliance via Getty Images; 155 (tr, cl, cr) Tomohiro Ohsumi/Getty Images; 156–157 Courtesy of Alain Sainz; 157 (cl) Created by Luis Fuentes; 158–159 Photography by Steph Distasio; 160 Photography by Steve Campbell and Matt Mamula; 161 (l) Photography by Steve Campbell and Matt Mamula, (r) Kelli Pearson/New Ground Technology/Cover Images; 164–165 Olivia Mears of @AvantGeek; 166 Petr Svarc/Alamy Stock Photo; 167 (t) Andrew Hasson/Getty Images, (bl, br) Tui De Roy/naturepl.com; 168 Caters News; 169 (tr) © Ewien van Bergeijk-Kwant/Solent News & Photo Agency; 170–171 Courtesy of Boris Toledo; 172 (bkg) ZUMA Press, Inc./Alamy Stock Photo, (bl, br) Putu Sayoga/Getty Images; 173 (t) Mercury Press via Caters News, (bl, br) Putu Sayoga/Getty Images, (b) © Flickr: Saint-Marcel-d'Ardèche, Wikimedia Commons//CC-BY-SA 3.0; 236 (t, b) Mercury Press/Michael Murphy/The Body Shop; 237 (t, c, b) Michael Steele/Getty Images; 238 (t) Tom and Debi Kline, (b) STR/AFP via Getty Images; 239 Caters News; 240 (t) John Cancalosi/naturepl.com, (cl) Ryu Uchiyama/Nature Production/Minden Pictures, (bl) Yasuda Mamoru/Nature Production/Minden Pictures, (br) Cagan Hakki Sekercioglu via Getty; 241 Courtesy of Laurie Wolf; 242 (t) Mercury Press, (cl) Randy Forsman /Mercury Press; 243 (t) Photo by Jane Barlow/PA Images via Getty Images, (cl) Photo by Jeff J Mitchell/Getty Images; MASTER GRAPHICS © KAMONRAT/Shutterstock.com, © Ornithopter/Shutterstock.com, © creativenv/Shutterstock.com, © best_vector/Shutterstock.com, © Olga Moonlight/Shutterstock.com; Icons made by Freepik, Kiranshastry, Vitaly Gorbachev, justicon, Smashicons, Zlatko Najdenovski, dDara, srip, Icongeek26, turkkub from www.flaticon.com; Icon made by Minh Do from www.iconfinder.com; Icon vector created by alvaro_cabrera from www.freepik.com; Icon made by Symbolicons from www.iconfinder.com/CC-BY-SA 3.0

Key: t = top, b = bottom, c = center, l = left, r = right, sp = single page, dp = double page, bkg = background

All other photos are from Ripley Entertainment Inc. Every attempt has been made to acknowledge correctly and contact copyright holders and we apologize in advance for any unintentional errors or omissions, which will be corrected in future editions.

Connect with Ripley's Online or in Person

31 MIND-BLOWING LOCATIONS

There are 31 incredible Ripley's Believe It or Not! Odditoriums all around the world, where you can experience our spectacular collection and have your mind blown!

Amsterdam THE NETHERLANDS

Atlantic City NEW JERSEY

Baltimore MARYLAND

Blackpool ENGLAND

Branson MISSOURI

Cavendish P.E.I., CANADA

Copenhagen DENMARK

Dubai UNITED ARAB EMIRATES

Gatlinburg TENNESSEE

Genting Highlands MALAYSIA

Grand Prairie TEXAS

Guadalajara MEXICO

Hollywood CALIFORNIA

Jeju Island KOREA

Key West FLORIDA

Mexico City MEXICO

Myrtle Beach SOUTH CAROLINA

New York City NEW YORK

Newport OREGON

Niagara Falls ONTARIO, CANADA

Ocean City MARYLAND

Orlando FLORIDA

Panama City Beach FLORIDA

Pattaya THAILAND

San Antonio TEXAS

San Francisco CALIFORNIA

St. Augustine FLORIDA

Surfers Paradise AUSTRALIA

Veracruz MEXICO

Williamsburg VIRGINIA

Wisconsin Dells WISCONSIN

Stop by our website daily for new stories, photos, contests, and more! **www.ripleys.com**
Don't forget to connect with us on social media for a daily dose of the weird and the wonderful.

/RipleysBelieveItOrNot   @Ripleys   youtube.com/Ripleys

@RipleysBelieveItorNot   @RipleysBelieveItorNot   @ripleysbelieveitornot

ALL NEW BOOKS FROM Ripley® PUBLISHING

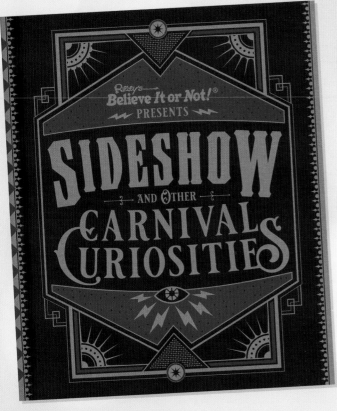

Learn the true stories behind some of the most fascinating acts in sideshow history and modern times!

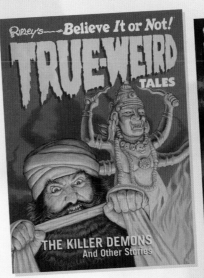

THE KILLER DEMONS
And Other Stories

THE DEVIL'S MIRROR
And Other Stories

From ghost stories based in truth to legends that leave you looking over your shoulder, *True-Weird Tales* boasts hand-drawn artwork by *Ripley's Believe It or Not!* cartoonist John Graziano. Each story and illustration captures the creepy, bringing these stranger-than fiction stories to life for kids who love to curl up with a spooky book.

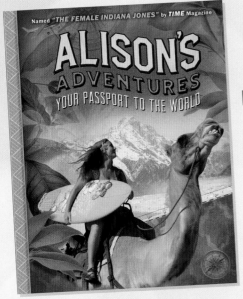

Get to know this "female Indiana Jones" through stories from her life exploring remote corners of the Earth, encountering exotic people and places, and investigating the world's greatest myths and legends!

In today's world, many misconceptions have been perpetuated—becoming modern day "facts." Ripley's puts those beliefs to the test and bursts the bubbles surrounding common delusions.

From the editors of Ripley's Believe It or Not! and IFL Science comes a book that will not only educate but entertain, giving a deeper approach to science and the wonders of the world around us.

www.ripleys.com/books

READING AND LEARNING WITH  PUBLISHING

Jump into all the weird, wild, and wacky stories and activities collected just for kids from the editors of Ripley's Believe It or Not!

How much trouble could one little girl get into exploring all by herself? Um, maybe a little...

What are all those twinkling lights in the night sky? Ponder the stars on a night swim with eagle ray Rosie.

 **Readers**
All true and unbelievable!

Designed to help kids build their reading skills and confidence at any level, this program offers a variety of fun, entertaining, and unbelievable topics to interest even the most reluctant readers.

LEVEL ONE Sounding it out
Sounding It Out
Preschool-Kindergarten
- learning sight words
- beginning reading
- sounding out words

LEVEL TWO Reading with help
Reading With Help
Preschool-Grade 1
- expanding vocabulary
- building confidence
- sounding out bigger words

LEVEL THREE Independent reading
Independent Reading
Grades 1-3
- introducing paragraphs
- challenging vocabulary
- reading for comprehension

LEVEL FOUR Chapters
Chapters
Grades 2-4
- reading for learning
- more complex content
- feeding curiosity